GENESIS:
Promises and Beginnings

JACK W. HAYFORD
Executive Editor

THOMAS NELSON
Since 1798

NASHVILLE   DALLAS   MEXICO CITY   RIO DE JANEIRO   BEIJING

Published in Nashville, Tennessee. Thomas Nelson is a registered trademark of Thomas Nelson, Inc.

Thomas Nelson, Inc., titles may be purchased in bulk for educational, business, fundraising, or sales promotional use. For information, please email SpecialMarkets@ThomasNelson.com.

Unless otherwise indicated, all Scripture quotations are from the New King James Version, copyright © 1982 by Thomas Nelson, Inc.

Hayford, Jack W.

Genesis: Promises and Beginnings

ISBN 13: 978-1-4185-4119-4

Printed in the United States of America
09 10 11 12 13 14 — 6 5 4 3 2

TABLE OF CONTENTS

QG 06-03-16

How Does Genesis Relate to Today?

GENESIS MAY BE the most read book of the Bible. Why? Anyone who decides to read the entire Bible usually makes it through the first book. We may be fairly familiar with its stories, but do we really understand its full message? What more can be learned from this book beyond the beginning of man and his early history?

Deep within the majestic stories of Genesis is a treasure trove of foundational truth. In the powerful characters and images contained in this opening volume we encounter our Creator and His perfect plan for His kingdom. In this book, as in no other, we come face-to-face with the Almighty and begin to experience the reality of His unconditional love.

Walking the Christian road can be very difficult and filled with obstacles. We can grow weary and sometimes misplace our hope. Genesis can lead us to new beginnings and the realization of endless promise. It points the way to a vibrant, dynamic relationship with our Creator. In its pages we discover the incredible promises that are ours as children of God—promises that held true yesterday and still hold true today and forever.

As you journey through this study, you will discover the intimate relationship God longs to have with you. You will see with fresh eyes how deeply you are loved and how faithful your Father is to answer whenever you call. His love, His promises, His faithfulness are everlasting. "As it was in the beginning, is now and ever shall be; world without end. Amen."

Keys of the Kingdom

KEYS CAN BE SYMBOLS of possession, of the right and ability to acquire, clarify, open, or ignite. Keys can be concepts that unleash mind-boggling possibilities. Keys clear the way to a possibility otherwise obstructed!

Jesus spoke of keys: "And I will give you the keys of the kingdom of heaven, and whatever you bind on earth will be bound in heaven, and whatever you loose on earth will be loosed in heaven" (Matthew 16:19).

While Jesus did not define the "keys" He has given, it is clear that He did confer upon His church specific tools that grant us access to a realm of spiritual "partnership" with Him. The "keys" are concepts or biblical themes, traceable throughout Scripture, that are verifiably dynamic when applied with solid faith under the lordship of Jesus Christ. The "partnership" is the essential feature of this enabling grace, allowing believers to receive Christ's promise of "kingdom keys," and to be assured of the Holy Spirit's readiness to actuate their power in the life of the believer.

Faithful students of the Word of God and some of today's most respected Christian leaders have noted some of the primary themes that undergird this spiritual partnership. A concise presentation of many of these primary themes can be found in the Kingdom Dynamics feature of the *New Spirit-Filled Life Bible.* The Spirit-Filled Life Study Guide series, an outgrowth of this Kingdom Dynamics feature, provides a treasury of more in-depth insights on these central truths. This study series offers challenges and insights designed to enable you to more readily understand and appropriate certain dynamic KINGDOM KEYS.

Each study guide has twelve to fourteen lessons, and a number of helpful features have been developed to assist you in your study, each marked by a symbol and heading for easy identification.

Kingdom Key

KINGDOM KEY identifies the foundational Scripture passage for each study session and highlights a basic concept or principle presented in the text along with cross-referenced passages.

Kingdom Life

The KINGDOM LIFE feature is designed to give practical under-standing and insight. This feature will assist you in comprehending the truths contained in Scripture and applying them to your day-to-day needs, hurts, relationships, concerns, or circumstances.

Word Wealth

The WORD WEALTH feature provides important definitions of key terms.

Behind the Scenes

BEHIND THE SCENES supplies information about cultural beliefs and practices, doctrinal disputes, and various types of background information that will illuminate Bible passages and teachings.

Kingdom Extra

The optional KINGDOM EXTRA feature will guide you to Bible dictionaries, Bible encyclopedias, and other resources that will enable you to gain further insight into a given topic.

Probing the Depths

Finally, PROBING THE DEPTHS will present any controversial issues raised by particular lessons and cite Bible passages and other sources that will assist you in arriving at your own conclusions.

Each volume of the Spirit-Filled Life Study Guide series is a com-prehensive resource presenting study and life-application questions and exercises with spaces provided for recording your answers. These study guides are designed to provide all you need to gain a good, basic understanding of the covered theme and apply biblical counsel to your life. You will need only a heart and mind open to the Holy Spirit, a prayerful attitude, a pencil, and a Bible to complete the studies and apply the truths they contain. However, you may want to have a notebook handy if you plan to expand your study to include the optional KINGDOM EXTRA feature.

The Bible study method used in this series employs four basic steps:

1. *Observation:* What does the text say?
2. *Interpretation:* What is the original meaning of the text?
3. *Correlation:* What light can be shed on this text by other Scripture passages?
4. *Application:* How should my life change in response to the Holy Spirit's teaching of this text?

The New King James Version is the translation used wherever Scripture portions are cited in the Spirit-Filled Life Study Guide series. Using this translation with this series will make your study easier, but it is certainly not imperative, and you will profit through the use of any translation you choose.

Through Bible study, you will grow in your essential understanding of the Lord, His kingdom, and your place in it; but you need more. Jesus was sent to teach us "all things" (John 14:25–26). Rely on the Holy Spirit to guide your study and your application of the Bible's truths. Bathe your study time in prayer as you use this series to learn of Him and His plan for your life. Ask the Spirit of God to illuminate the text, enlighten your mind, humble your will, and comfort your heart. And as you explore the Word of God and find the keys to unlock its riches, may the Holy Spirit fill every fiber of your being with the joy and power God longs to give all His children. Read diligently on. Stay open and submissive to Him. Learn to live your life as the Creator intended. You will not be disappointed. He promises you!

ADDITIONAL OBSERVATIONS

INTRODUCTION

Genesis: The Foundation

Kingdom Life—*Fitting All the Pieces*

MANY PEOPLE love to work jigsaw puzzles. Finding where each piece fits is a challenge which brings a feeling of victory with every bit of color that finds its true home. As each tiny piece is connected, all the mysterious shapes and colors begin to align and recognizable images begin to emerge. But problems are encountered when the most definite shapes and colors have been connected and only the pieces that are not easily identifiable are left. Blue could be sea or sky, green could be grass or trees, and dark shadows remain mysterious. It is at this point in the process that many concede defeat and the puzzle scene in all its splendor is never revealed.

For many people studying the Old Testament is like an adventure in working a jigsaw puzzle. There are some stories in there that are familiar from Sunday school days, like the bright patches of color in the puzzle scene. In between the familiar stories are long stretches of unfamiliar narrative and lists of names that seem as featureless as the sky or the grass, or as illusive as unknown shadows in the puzzle.

Just as in working a jigsaw puzzle, creating a framework for your Bible study is the best place to start. Before you tackle Genesis, looking for the bright patches of familiar stories, let's construct the framework so you can see how the whole composition goes together to convey a message from God to the children of Israel in days gone by and from God to you today.

Behind the Scenes

The Hebrew Bible has a simple way of naming its first five books. It uses the first word of each book as the name. What we call "Genesis" is named *Bereshith,* which means "in the beginning." When the Old Testament was translated into Greek about 250 years before Christ, these books were given formal titles that reflected their content. The first book was titled *Genesis*, a Greek word for "origins" or "history." This Greek name has become the standard name for the first book of the Old Testament in English translations.

Probing the Depths

Genesis presents itself anonymously. No author's name or date of composition is attached. But Genesis is the background every Israelite needed in order to understand his or her national history as recorded in the Pentateuch: Genesis, Exodus, Leviticus, Numbers, and Deuteronomy. These five books go together.

Read Exodus 17:14; 24:4, 7; Numbers 33:1–2; Deuteronomy 31:9–13; Leviticus 1:1; Luke 16:29, 31; John 5:45–47.

Questions:

To whom did Jesus attribute the writing of the Pentateuch?

_____

_____

How many years before King Solomon built the temple did Moses lead the Israelites out of Egypt (1 Kings 6:1)?

_____

The fourth year of Solomon's reign was approximately 996 B.C. What was the approximate date of the exodus?

_____

If Moses compiled Genesis sometime during the forty years the Israelites wandered in the wilderness, what would be the latest it could have been written?

_____

(Remember, when you move backward in time dated B.C., the numbers get larger, and when you move forward, the numbers get smaller.)

The Structure of Genesis

To understand Genesis, it is best divided into three unequal parts. Chapters 1—11 recount the spiritual history of the human race from creation to the time of Abraham. These chapters reveal how the physical and social worlds came to be. They also explain to us why God called out one man and began dealing in a unique way with his descendants. The second section (chapters 12—36) tells how God selected Abraham, Isaac, and Jacob to initiate His chosen people. And the third section (chapters 37—50) details how God purified the sons of Jacob to serve as patriarchs for the tribes of the nation of Israel. The last two sections tell the stories of the ancestors of Israel up to the time they moved to Egypt.

Kingdom Life—*Understanding God's Kingdom*

God the Creator

Genesis chapters 1—11 reveal to the seeking heart the faithful Creator whose love transcends the faithlessness of men and women.

To understand the kingdom of God, it is necessary to begin with Genesis. It is here that we first meet the Sovereign of the universe. At the outset His realm, reign, and regency are described. In the first few passages of the Bible, we learn that His realm (or the scope of His rule) is transcendent; that is, not only does it include the entire physical universe, but it exceeds it. He existed before all creation, He expands beyond it, and by virtue of having begotten it, He encompasses all that it is. It is in this beginning book that we learn that God's reign (the power by which He rules) is exercised by His will, His word, and His works. By His own will He creatively decides and designs; by His own word He speaks creation into being; and by His own works His Spirit displays His unlimited power. Genesis reveals God's regency (His authority to rule). God alone is preexistent and holy. He is there before creation "in the beginning." Thus, as its Creator, He deserves to be its Potentate. His benevolent intent in creating "good" things reveals His holy nature (complete and perfect) and thus His moral right to be creation's King. All kingdom power and authority flow from Him.

Read Genesis 1:1–31; 4:1–15; 6:13–22; 8:20—9:17; 10:1–32.

Questions:

In what ways does God reveal His faithfulness to you in these passages?

✎ _____

_____

_____

What assurances do these passages give you?

✎ _____

_____

God the Redeemer

In Genesis chapters 12—36, God reveals Himself as the God who enters into a covenant with a chosen family of faith.

The promise of God to Abraham that he would be "heir of the world" (Romans 4:13) is repeated to his offspring, Isaac and Jacob, in succession. God's words and dealings in the lives of the patriarchs reveal that His unfolding program of redemption is dual: He not only provides for restored fellowship with Himself (relationship), but covenants for human fulfillment and personal fruitfulness in life. This plan is geared not only to bless His people, but to make them a blessing to others.

Read Genesis 11:31—12:9; 15:1–21; 17:1–27; 18:16–33; 21:1–21; 22:1–19; 24:1–67; 25:19–34; 28:10–22; 31:3–18; 32:9–32; 35:1–15.

Questions:

For each passage listed above, write down God's action to initiate or preserve a relationship with His chosen family.

✎ _____

_____

_____

_____

_____

What effect do these actions have on you today?

_____

_____

God the Sanctifier

The meaning and process of sanctification is unveiled in Genesis chapters 37—50.

Although Jacob was a man of absolute faith in the Lord who had revealed Himself at Bethel and blessed his life, he was also a deceitful man who raised a family of treacherous and violent sons. (See Genesis 34.) Before God would build a nation of the twelve sons of Jacob, He set out to make godly men of them through suffering.

Read Genesis 37:12–35; 38:1–26; 39:1—40:23; 42:1–24; 42:36—43:15; 45:1–15; 46:1–34; 50:15–21.

Questions:

What is revealed about wicked character?

_____

_____

How can righteousness be produced by suffering?

_____

_____

How have you experienced the process of sanctification in your own life?

_____

_____

Word Wealth—*Sanctified*

Sanctified: Greek *hagiadzo* (hag-ee-ad'-zoe); Strong's #37: God the Father sanctified Jesus, and the Holy Spirit performs a work of sanctification in the lives of individual believers. The word *hagiadzo* means to "hallow," "set apart," "dedicate," "consecrate," "separate," "sanctify," "make holy." *Hagiadzo* as a state of holiness is opposite of *koinon,* "common" or "unclean." In the Old Testament things, places, and ceremonies were named *hagiadzo.* Because His Father set Him apart, Jesus is appropriately called the Holy One (Luke 1:35). The Holy Spirit is at work in the life of each believer sanctifying him or her. It is God's desire to enter every aspect of a person's life and fill it with Himself. A person is sanctified when he commits every aspect of his life exclusively to the Lord. A person who is sanctified by God's Holy Spirit is set free at the deepest dimensions of his life and is released into fruitfulness.

Record Your Thoughts

The Lord is the Creator. He is the God of beginnings. And He is the Lord of promises. He is ever faithful to His creatures who come to Him in faith for deliverance from eternal punishment for sin and from the power of sin in their daily lives.

Questions:

What are some examples of how the Lord has been a faithful Creator to you, protecting and preserving your physical existence?

_____

_____

_____

What are some examples of how the Lord has assured you of His faithfulness, maintaining His relationship with you as your Savior and Lord?

_____

_____

_____

What are some examples of how the Lord has worked faithfully in and through the difficulties of your life, building holiness in your character?

_____

_____

_____

SESSION ONE

The Beginning of All

Genesis 1:1—2:25

Kingdom Key—*God Created All Things*

Revelation 4:11 You are worthy, O Lord, to receive glory and honor and power; for You created all things, and by Your will they exist and were created.

Genesis immediately brings into question many secular world-views, so serious Genesis students must become accustomed to thinking differently. We must perceive the world and its history as the ancient biblical authors revealed it. The opening narratives are not to be understood allegorically but as actual history.

God is the Father of all creation, the Creator of all. He is all-powerful and sustains the universe. He exists outside the universe (theologians call this transcendence), yet He is present throughout the universe (theologians say He is immanent) and is its ruler. He exists in nature, but He is not nature, nor is He bound by the laws of nature as the pantheists (those who believe that God and the material world are one and/or who believe in multiple deities) assert. He is the source of all life and everything that is.

The best description of God is the name that He gave for Himself to the early Israelites, *Yahweh*. *Yahweh* is usually translated "Jehovah" or "Lord." Scholars believe that this Hebrew verb "to be" literally means "He who causes (everything else) to be."

The Word of God must always stand above the word of man; we are not to judge His Word, but rather, it judges us.

Word Wealth—*Created*

Created: Hebrew *bara'* (bah-rah'); Strong's #1254: To form or fashion, to produce, to create. Originally this verb carried the idea of "carving" or "cutting out." This suggests that creating is similar to sculpting. Thus *bara'* is a fitting word to describe both creating by bringing into existence and creating by fashioning existing matter into something new, as God did in creating man out of the dust from the ground. God is always the subject of the verb *bara'* in its standard form; creating is therefore a divine capacity. By reserving this word to describe God's creativity, the Scripture makes clear that divine and human creativity are different. The noblest human creation is but a distant echo of the original divine one described in Genesis 1 and 2.

Kingdom Life—*God Brings Order*

"The earth was without form, and void; and darkness was on the face of the deep" (Genesis 1:2). By this we should understand that the earth was lacking the order it would have when God's commands were complete. Both these statements reveal that the act of creation reflects God's normal process of bringing order out of chaos.

Read Isaiah 40.

Questions:

What does this chapter reveal to you about God's desire to bring order out of chaos?

_____

_____

_____

How does this aspect of God's nature impact your spiritual life?

_____

_____

_____

Kingdom Extra

The creation is an important biblical theme in more places than Genesis. Many passages in the Old Testament give us deeper insight into the creation story. From them we can glean a more personal application and a greater understanding of the implication of creation for our relationship with God.

Read Job 38; Psalm 104; Isaiah 42:5–6.

Questions:

What can you learn from these passages about the personal relationship God desires with you?

_____

_____

_____

What attitudes must be cultivated in order to obtain this relationship?

_____

_____

_____

The Trinity in Creation

Father, Son, and Holy Spirit were present and active at creation. To think otherwise is to misunderstand the nature of the triune God.

The Trinity is one of the great theological mysteries. There are some who think that because we believe in monotheism, one God, we cannot accept the concept of the Trinity. Yet the Bible teaches that the Godhead consists of three divine persons—Father, Son, and Holy Spirit—each fully God, each showing fully the divine nature (Luke 3:21–22).

The Father is the fountainhead of the Trinity, the Creator, the First Cause. He is the primary thought, the concept of all that has been and will be created. Jesus said, "My Father has been working until now, and I have been working" (John 5:17).

The Son is the *Logos* or expression of God—the "only begotten"

(John 1:14) of the Father—and He Himself is God. Further, as God incarnate, He reveals the Father to us (John 14:9–11). The Son of God is both the agent of creation and mankind's only Redeemer.

The Holy Spirit, the third person of the Trinity, proceeds from the Father and is worshipped and glorified together with the Father and the Son. He inspired the Scriptures, empowers God's people, and convicts the world "of sin, and of righteousness, and of judgment" (John 16:8). During creation, "the Spirit of God was hovering over the face of the waters" (Genesis 1:2).

All three persons of the Godhead are eternal. The Father exists and has existed forever. With Him always existed His expression, the Son. Always the Father loved the Son, and the Son loved and served the Father. From that relationship of love proceeds the Spirit of God, who is eternal and has existed forever. The Father did not exist first, then later the Son, and still later the Spirit. They all three have existed from before there was anything that could begin—three distinct persons all functioning as One.

Read 1 Corinthians 12:4–6; 2 Corinthians 13:14; Ephesians 4:4–6; 2 Thessalonians 2:13–14.

Questions:

Express in your own words the meaning of *Trinitarian God.*

_____

_____

_____

How is each "personhood" of God experienced in your own life?

_____

_____

_____

How was the Son of God involved in creation? (See John 1:1–13; Colossians 1:15–20; Hebrews 1:1–3.)

_____

_____

_____

What impact does this have on your life today?

✎_____

_____

_____

The Form and Filling

The six creative days address the problem that "the earth was without form, and void" (Genesis 1:2). In other words, the earth was shapeless and empty. In the first three days God created the "forms," the broad categories of existence. In the second three days, God addressed the emptiness of the earth by populating the vacant forms of the first three days.

Fill out the following chart by listing what God spoke into existence each day. Notice the relationships between days one through three and days four through six of the creative week.

FORM	FILLING
Day 1	*Day 4*
✎_____	_____
_____	_____
_____	_____
(Genesis 1:3–5)	(Genesis 1:14–19)
Day 2	*Day 5*
✎_____	_____
_____	_____
_____	_____
(Genesis 1:6–8)	(Genesis 1:20–23)
Day 3	*Day 6*
✎_____	_____
_____	_____
_____	_____
(Genesis 1:9–13)	(Genesis 1:24–31)

The Sixth Day

God formed the earth, the sky, and the sea. He placed the sun, moon, and stars in their place. He filled the earth with living creatures and declared all was good. Then God created Adam.

The Hebrew word 'adam is translated twenty times in the Old Testament as the proper name "Adam." It is translated more than five hundred times as "man." As with the English word "man," 'adam in its general sense has nothing to do with maleness and everything to do with humanness.

Read Genesis 1:27–30.

Questions:

What do these verses reveal about humankind's relationship to the image of God?

_____

_____

_____

What do these verses reveal about humankind's relationship to the earth?

_____

_____

_____

What impact should God's original plan have on your day-to-day life?

_____

_____

_____

Kingdom Extra

"The image of God" (Genesis 1:27) that men and women bear does not involve physical appearance. It has to do with personality and the ability to form loving, committed relationships with other people and with God.

"God" in Genesis 1 is both singular and plural (v. 26), and so is "man" (v. 27). Men and women bear God's image individually, but in loving, committed relationships they show the complexity of God and humanity. A loving, committed marriage and family are a full expression of God's image.

Kingdom Life—*Reach for the Heights*

Man is distinct from the rest of creation. The Divine Triune Counsel determined that man was to have God's image and likeness. Man is a spiritual being who is not only body, but also soul and spirit. He is a moral being whose intelligence, perception, and self-determination far exceed that of any other earthly being.

These properties or traits possessed by humankind and his prominence in the order of creation imply the intrinsic worth, not only of humankind, but also of each human individual.

Capacity and ability constitute accountability and responsibility. We should never be pleased to dwell on a level of existence lower than that on which God has made it possible for us to dwell. We should strive to be the best we can be and to reach the highest levels we can reach. To do less is to be unfaithful stewards of the life entrusted to us.

Read Psalms 8:4–8; 139:13–16.

Questions:

What do these verses reveal to you about your "destiny" and God's plan for your life?

_____

_____

_____

What has God formed within you that you have yet to embrace and possess?

_____

_____

_____

Establishing a Relationship

After surveying the grand sweep of the creation of the universe and all living things, Moses focused in on the details of the creation of the first man and the first woman. Genesis 1:26–30 provides the theology of human creation. Genesis 2:4–25 gives us a tour of their home and a personal introduction.

Questions:

Notice the change in names for deity. What divine name appears consistently in Genesis 1:1—2:3?

✎_____

This is a name of power.

What divine name appears consistently in Genesis 2:4—3:24?

✎_____

This compound name adds God's relational name to His name of power.

Genesis 2:4—3:24 stresses God's intimate relationship with His human creatures. Complete the chart below to show how Genesis 2:5–6 parallels Genesis 1:2 in showing the need for divine intervention.

Genesis 1:2	Genesis 2:5–6
The earth was without form, and void; and darkness was on the face of the deep. And the Spirit of God was hovering over the face of the waters.	✎_____ _____ _____ _____

A Unique Destiny

Having been made of the dust of the ground, a human being is as any other creature—a biological entity. The creaturely existence, however, is insufficient to describe the human being. Man became the crowning act of creation and is distinguished as being different—*God literally breathed life into man!*

Unlike the rest of creation, a human being has been created in a covenant relationship with God and has an exceptionally high and distinct value and destiny. The likeness of man to the Creator is in the form and function of personal unity. God designed the human personality to consist of self-consciousness and self-determination, with both the freedom and the awareness to respond to God, to other human beings, and to the environment. He also designed a destiny for man far higher and nobler than that of any other creature. When God said, "Let Us make man in Our image, according to Our likeness" (Genesis 1:26), He had planned from the foundation of the world a glorious future for those who would choose the redeeming grace of Jesus Christ.

Read Genesis 2:7–17.

Questions:

Describe man's original relationship with God.

_____

_____

_____

What was God's plan for man with regard to his environment?

_____

_____

_____

What attitude or state of heart changed the way man interacted with God and the world?

_____

_____

_____

What does this mean for your life today?

_____

_____

_____

Distinct and Equal

When God presented the woman to Adam, Adam immediately recognized something of himself in her. She was part of him; in effect, his "other self." God then instructed that they should "be joined" (cleave) and "become one flesh" (Genesis 2:24). Their unity was to be so complete that the Hebrew word for "one" (*'echad*) is the same word used to describe God in Deuteronomy 6:4: "The LORD our God, the LORD is one!" It was not until the entrance of sin that their unity was broken, their relationship became contentious, and they took on separate identities.

Read Ephesians 5:21–32.

Questions:

In what way does a godly relationship between husband and wife reveal the proper way in which to relate to others? To God?

✎_____

_____

_____

What do you believe is the "great mystery" (Ephesians 5:32) of which Paul speaks?

✎_____

_____

_____

Record Your Thoughts

Since a full relationship with God has been reinstated through the sacrifice of Jesus, what personal promises can you discover through Adam's original relationship with God?

✎_____

_____

_____

_____

SESSION TWO

The Beginning of Sin

Genesis 3:1—5:32

Kingdom Key—*All Have Sinned*

Romans 5:12 Just as through one man sin entered the world, and death through sin, and thus death spread to all men, because all sinned.

Original sin is the term used to refer to the first sin by the first sinners. Usually when theologians refer to original sin, they are interested in how the very first sin corrupts every descendant of the original sinners.

Is original sin's effect on humankind an inherited spiritual defect that makes people guilty before each of them commits his or her own sins? Or is the effect of original sin on the human race only an inherited weakness toward temptation, so that every person is spiritually innocent until he or she sins personally and earns his or her guilt?

Read Romans 3:23; Galatians 3:22.

Questions:

How do you understand "original sin"?

_____

_____

_____

What evidence supports your view?

_____

_____

_____

How has original sin impacted your life?

✎ _____

_____

_____

Kingdom Life—*Recognize Sin*

The first woman and the first man chose evil. They didn't stumble into sin because they were bored and had nothing better to do. For a moment, evil looked good and death looked like life itself, but then they experienced sin's betrayal just as their descendants have ever since.

The message to us in this is that we must recognize sin. In order to do that, we must know exactly what it is.

Read 1 John 3:4–24.

Questions:

Based on this passage, how do you define sin?

✎ _____

_____

What is its cause?

✎ _____

_____

What is the effect of sin?

✎ _____

_____

_____

What has been the effect of sin in your own life?

✎ _____

_____

_____

Word Wealth—*Sin*

Sin: Greek *hamartia* (ham-ar-tee'-ah); Strong's #*266*: Literally "missing the mark," failure, offense, taking the wrong course, wrongdoing, guilt. The New Testament uses the word in a generic sense for concrete wrongdoing (John 8:34, 46; 2 Corinthians 11:7; James 1:15); as a principle and quality of action (Romans 5:12, 13, 20; Hebrews 3:13); and as a sinful deed (Matthew 12:31; Acts 7:60; 1 John 5:16).

Probing the Depths

Humankind was created without sin, morally upright, and inclined to do good (Ecclesiastes 7:29). But sin entered into human experience when Adam and Eve violated the direct command of God by eating the forbidden fruit in the garden of Eden (Genesis 3:6). Adam was the head and representative of the whole human race; therefore, his sin affected all future generations (Romans 5:12–21). Associated with this guilt is a fallen nature passed from Adam to all his descendants. Out of this fallen nature, twisted from the original order of God's benevolent intent, arise all the sins that people commit (Matthew 15:19); no person is free from involvement in sin (Romans 3:23).

Read Psalm 119:160; James 2:10; Ephesians 2:1.

Questions:

Based on these Scriptures, what is your definition of sin?

_____

_____

Is any sin minor? Why?

_____

_____

What happens when one continues in sin?

_____

_____

_____

Is there a sin in your own life you struggle to resist?

_____

_____

What is the result in your life?

_____

_____

The Look of Temptation

What is it in human nature—a nature God created—that makes us susceptible to temptation or vulnerable to sin? Adam and Eve were created apart from sin and without the need to sin, yet some characteristic in their makeup allowed sin to enter their lives.

Eve made the choice to believe a lie. This was the doorway through which sin entered her life (Genesis 3:13; 2 Corinthians 11:3; 1 Timothy 2:14). Adam chose to ignore God's voice of authority (Genesis 3:17). These two choices—self-deception and self-will—are actually two sides of the same coin. Both remain as complicating realities in our own lives today, allowing sin to continue to take root and bear its deadly fruit in us—*until* Christ enters our lives and breaks the bonds of sin, empowering us to resist it.

Temptation is sin's call to our basic needs and desires to be satisfied in self-serving or perverted ways. It is also a call to practice self-deception, finding ways to justify doing as we please, even though we know in our heart of hearts that doing as we please is wrong.

Read Mark 7:21–23; 1 John 2:16.

Questions:

What is the end result in a heart filled with self-service?

_____

_____

Do you ever see signs of this in your own life? How do they make themselves evident?

_____

_____

What actions can you take to end the sinful effects of this heart attitude?

✎_____

_____

The Way of the Tempter

There are very few references to the "tempter" in Scripture. One of them is in Genesis 3.

Let's take a closer look at the whole scenario. Write in this chart the ways in which the man and the woman were tempted, how they resisted, and their motivations as you see them.

THE WOMAN	THE MAN
Temptation:	
✎_____	_____
_____	_____
_____	_____
_____	_____
_____	_____
Resistance:	
✎_____	_____
_____	_____
_____	_____
_____	_____
_____	_____
Motivation:	
✎_____	_____
_____	_____
_____	_____
_____	_____
_____	_____

Questions:

What other references can you find to the "tempter" in Scripture?

_____

_____

_____

What do these reveal about the Enemy of our souls?

_____

_____

_____

What feelings did the Serpent attempt to evoke in Eve?

_____

_____

_____

What do Eve's responses tell you about her thoughts toward God?

_____

_____

_____

How might recognizing Adam's and Eve's faulty responses help you guard your heart from temptation?

_____

_____

_____

According to Romans 5:12, the man, not the woman, brought sin into the human race. Why is he the responsible party for rebelling against God?

_____

_____

_____

Kingdom Life—*Sin Involves Consequences*

The Serpent told the woman that the results of eating of the tree would be that she would "be like God, knowing good and evil" (Genesis 3:5). The actual results were far different.

Before sin, the man and the woman enjoyed an openness toward the Lord God and one another without shame or fear (Genesis 2:25). After sin, they were instinctively defensive and filled with shame and fear.
Read Genesis 3:8–16.

Questions:

What evidence was immediate when the first man and woman became separated from God?

_____

_____

_____

Why do you think this was?

_____

_____

_____

Compare Adam's confession and Eve's confession. What differences do you see?

_____

_____

_____

What does this tell us with regard to our own sin and repentance?

_____

_____

_____

In your opinion was it punishment or mercy on the Lord God's part to prevent Adam and Eve from living endlessly? Why?

✎ _____

_____

_____

Behind the Scenes

Genesis 3:15 contains the first proclamation of the gospel. All of the richness, the mercy, the sorrow, and the glory of God's redeeming work with man is here in miniature. God promises to bring a Redeemer from the seed of the woman; He will be completely human yet divinely begotten. "That serpent of old, called the Devil," (Revelation 12:9) would war with the Seed and would smite Him. (See Revelation 12.) But even as the Serpent struck at His heel, His foot would descend and crush the Serpent's head.

In Christ's life and death this Scripture was fulfilled. Divinely begotten, yet fully human, He—by His death and resurrection—has defeated and made a public spectacle of the powers of hell (Colossians 2:15). This first messianic promise is one of the most succinct statements of the gospel to be found anywhere.

The Violence of Sin

The Lord God warned that sin would lead to immediate death (Genesis 2:17). The Serpent scoffed at the Lord God as a cosmic killjoy and predicted that the woman would become like God if she had the nerve to disobey Him. Adam and Eve did sin, but they did not become like God. They died spiritually, and their offspring began spilling blood all over the earth. According to Genesis, violence is the visible symptom of the disease of sin.

The choice of humankind to follow sin's temptation or obey God is never pictured more clearly than in the case of Cain and Abel. Even when God gave instruction to Cain as to how to effectively deal with his emotional state, Cain rejected God. His choice was ruled by his own desires. Violence was the result.

Read through chapters 4 and 5 of Genesis. Pay close attention to the choices made by each successive generation.

Questions:

What makes anger such a difficult emotion with which to do anything constructive?

_____

_____

_____

What makes you angry?

_____

_____

_____

What is one thing that makes you angry to the point of violence?

_____

_____

_____

How do you need to handle this temptation to violence with the help of God's grace?

_____

_____

_____

Kingdom Life—*God Is Faithful*

Through disobedience to the terms of God's rule, man "fell," thus experiencing the loss of his dominion. Everything within his delegated realm (the earth) came under a curse as his relationship with God, the fountainhead of his power to rule, was severed. Thus man lost the life-power essential to rule in God's kingdom. Beyond the tragedy of man's loss, two other facts unfold. First, through his disobedience to God and submission to the Serpent's suggestions, man's rule was forfeited to the

Serpent. (Revelation 12:9 verifies that the spirit employing the Serpent's form was Satan himself.) The domain originally delegated to man fell to Satan, who became administrator of this now-cursed realm. The Serpent's "seed" and "head" indicate a continual line (seed) of evil offspring extending Satan's rule (head). However, a second fact offers hope. Amid the tragedy of this sequence of events, God began to move redemptively, and a plan for recovering man's lost estate is now promised.

Behind the Scenes

While Eve was deceived by the Serpent and the first to violate the divine regulations set by God, the Word of God holds Adam as the disobedient one who knowingly broke trust with God. This fact does not intimate that the woman was less intelligent or more vulnerable to deception than the man, but that under the circumstances in which the Fall of man occurred, deception of the woman preceded *active disobedience* of the man.

It is a remarkable token of divine grace that God, in His mercy and in His giving of the first promise of a Deliverer/Messiah (Genesis 3:15), chose to bring this about by the seed of the woman. In short, the one first scarred by sin is selected to be the one first promised to become an instrument of God's redemptive work.

The birth of Seth, the "seed" given to replace the murdered Abel, was the first in the bloodline that would trace its way to the birth of the Lord Jesus Christ. Eve's distinct place in the failure of the first couple becomes the very soil in which God's mercy plants the first seed of promise. The message is obvious: God is able to "make all grace abound" (2 Corinthians 9:8) toward any of us. However deep the failure, Eve's testimony declares God's grace goes deeper still.

Read 2 Corinthians 9:8.

Question:

How have you experienced God's grace in your own life?

_____

_____

_____

Probing the Depths—*What Is the Unpardonable Sin?*

The concept of an unpardonable sin has been a source of difficulty for many because it seems to go against the Bible's teachings about grace. We understand that God's grace forgives every sin, but our Lord mentioned one sin that cannot be forgiven.

This concept is derived from Matthew 12:31. The religious leaders had come out to hear Jesus, but they opposed virtually everything He said. As He was casting out demons, they accused Him of doing this by satanic means.

Those people were so blind spiritually that they were attributing the work of the Holy Spirit to Satan. Furthermore, they were rejecting the Holy Spirit's work in their own lives. In essence, the Holy Spirit was saying of Jesus, "This is the Son of God. This is God," and they were saying, "He is not God! He is Satan's agent." It was then Jesus said, "Every sin and blasphemy will be forgiven men, but the blasphemy against the Spirit will not be forgiven" (Matthew 12:31).

Obviously, the unpardonable sin is not merely saying an unkind thing about the Holy Spirit. The religious leaders involved had turned totally against the revelation of God. They were so far into their own wickedness that they rejected not only Jesus Christ but also the Holy Spirit. They were saying that good was evil and evil was good. They called the Spirit of God, Satan!

Once they had rejected Jesus, the one source of forgiveness, there was now no forgiveness. A person who turns away from Jesus Christ can receive no forgiveness, and that is what they had done.

If you want to obey God but are concerned that you may have committed the unpardonable sin, you have not committed it. If anyone today has committed this sin, it would be one who is hard-hearted, who has turned against Jesus, reviled Him, and become so depraved that he would claim that God's Spirit is Satan.

Record Your Thoughts

Questions:

What factors do you think affect how an unbeliever expresses his sin nature in his behavior?

_____
_____
_____
_____
_____

What factors do you think influence how a born-again Christian expresses his sin nature in his behavior?

_____
_____
_____
_____
_____

How and why does sinful behavior cause you to withdraw from God and avoid contact with Him?

_____
_____
_____
_____
_____

Do you tend to place blame on people or circumstances for sin in your life?

_____
_____

How might honest confession change this?

_____
_____
_____
_____

The Beginning of Judgment

Genesis 6:1—9:29

Kingdom Key—*God Is Just*

Psalm 75:7 God is the Judge; He puts down one, and exalts another.

George had never been in a federal courtroom before. The courtroom was filled with friends and family, many from the church of which George was a member. They were there in support of a Christian brother who had embezzled a significant amount of money from work and confessed when he was about to be exposed. That was nothing to be proud of, but when the moment came, the brother had faced his guilt squarely before God, his employers, and his church. Now the trial was over and it was time for sentencing.

George's church family had presented a very heartfelt plea for leniency. After a good deal of formal judicial ritual, the robed judge addressed the defendant. "The presence of so many community members in the courtroom today testifies to the esteem in which many hold you. I have read the appeals of many of these same individuals who have asked me to consider the punishment you have already endured in the loss of position and respect in your profession and civic standing. They have asked me to take into account the pain the sentence of this court will cause your family.

"And while this court is not insensitive to the losses you and your family are going through, this court will not be swayed by them. It is you, and not this court, who have inflicted these wounds on yourself and on your family. This court bears not a whit of responsibility for them.

"This court imposes the following penalties . . ." But George was no longer listening to the details. His conscious mind had been overwhelmed by the stern majesty of unyielding justice. And when the scope of the sentence finally sank in, he wondered if the sentence of the judge wouldn't be easier to handle than the self-induced process of reaping what you sow. He felt sorry for his ashen-faced and tearful family.

Questions:

What about this story do you find difficult to accept?

_____

_____

_____

What might you learn about God from this story?

_____

_____

_____

What might you learn about your own actions from this story?

_____

_____

_____

Kingdom Life—*Sin Imposes Consequences*

All people have sinned, the Bible says, and no one naturally seeks after God as He really is. Just as in the story of George, no positive act on the part of any man can outweigh the devastating effect of sin. Where sin exists, a sure penalty must be paid. Since all have sinned, a penalty is leveled against all.

Although Adam's son Seth fathered many who desired to know and serve God, sin led humankind headlong toward judgment.
Read Romans 3:10–12, 23; 5:12–21; 6:23.

Questions:

What is God's grace?

✎_____

_____

_____

How do you understand "the gift of righteousness" (Romans 5:17)?

✎_____

_____

_____

In the story about George, what difference in the verdict would the "free gift" (Romans 5:16) of justification have made?

✎_____

_____

_____

How have you experienced this justification in your own life?

✎_____

_____

_____

Probing the Depths

The phrases "the sons of God" and "the daughters of men" in Genesis 6:1–4 can be difficult to understand. The view of the early church fathers was that "the sons of God" were angels who interbred with human women and by doing so incurred a special divine judgment. The expression "sons of God" usually refers to angels in the Old Testament (Job 1:6; 2:1). The passages about imprisoned angels in 1 Peter 3:19–20; 2 Peter 2:4, and Jude 6 (all verses precede references to the Flood) support this view.

The medieval view is that "the sons of God" and "daughters of men" are poetic references to the two branches of Adam's descendants in chapters 4 and 5. Once the godly line chose to intermarry with the godless line, the Lord's patience expired and He initiated the process of judgment.

The fallen angel view is linguistically superior and better explains the Lord's disgust and anger over the inappropriateness of angels approaching women. The view about the two lines of the human race better fits the preceding context. It is also more consistent with the teaching of Jesus that angels do not (note: not "cannot," but "are not to") engage in sexual activity (Matthew 22:30).

You may wish to locate commentaries and other trusted sources to learn more about this controversial passage.

Word Wealth—*Grace*

Grace: Hebrew *chen* (chayn); Strong's #2580: Favor, grace, graciousness, kindness, beauty, pleasantness, charm, attractiveness, loveliness, affectionate regard. The root *chanan* means "to act graciously or mercifully toward someone; to be compassionate, to be favorably inclined."

"Noah found **grace** [*chen*] in the eyes of the LORD" (Genesis 6:8, emphasis added). The Hebrew term *chen* is usually translated "favor" in the Old Testament. Usually "favor" is not a theological concept but a social one involving people helping people. In addition, the focus is not on the giver of the favor but on the receiver. Noah had been prepared by the Lord God through his father and family traditions (Genesis 5:29) to receive God's favor.

Kingdom Life—*God's Grace Is Sufficient*

In the New Testament the word translated "grace" is the Greek word *charis* (khar'-ece). It means unmerited favor, undeserved blessing, or a free gift. Its meaning is identical to that of the Hebrew *chen* of the Old Testament. It is God's favor; God's *unmerited* favor. It is a manifestation of His power, exceeding what we could achieve or hope for by our own labors. It is in mighty effect at our salvation, but it is also a God-given resource that makes a holy life possible when our life, circumstance, or character is under Satan's fire. God's grace becomes His enablement or empowerment to achieve His plan, endure hardship, or access Him. His grace facilitates our abilities to conquer every weakness as we yield to an absolute trust or reliance upon God, trusting His heart even when we cannot trace His hand.

Read 2 Corinthians 12:9; Ephesians 3:20; James 4:6.

Questions:

How have you experienced the activity of the Spirit of God in your life while striving against sin?

_____

_____

_____

Tell about a time when you experienced God's unmerited favor.

_____

_____

_____

What lasting effect did this have on your life?

_____

_____

_____

Word Wealth—*Covenant*

Covenant: Hebrew *berit* (beh-reet'); Strong's #1285: A covenant, compact, pledge, treaty, agreement. This is one of the most theologically important words in the Bible, appearing more than 250 times in the Old Testament. A *berit* may be made between individuals, between a king and his people, or by God with His people. Usually both parties commit themselves to doing something for their mutual benefit, but often when God is involved, He is the One who commits to action while people are the ones who benefit.

Genesis 6:18 contains the first use of the word "covenant" in the Bible. In this covenant God pledged that He would deliver Noah's family and a sampling of all the animals. Noah's part was to build the ark (vv. 14, 22).

The Judgment on Humankind

The Lord determined that humanity had become so corrupt that He had to destroy it. God's many facets of protection of Noah throughout the cataclysmic events of the Flood were His first installments of His covenant promise.

The Flood began when "the fountains of the great deep were broken up" (Genesis 7:11). Worldwide undersea earthquakes and volcanic eruptions occurred almost simultaneously, throwing massive ocean waves surging back and forth across the earth. It is considered by some that this may also refer to the cataclysm that created the continents by separating and spreading these giant landmasses from the original single landmass. The intense, prolonged downpour of rain, coupled with the massive water surges, resulted in the total flooding of the earth. According to Genesis 7:20, even the peaks of the highest mountains were covered by at least twenty-two feet of water.

 Behind the Scenes

The original order of man's environment on the earth must be distinguished from what it became following the impact of man's fall, the Curse, and the eventual Deluge. The agricultural, zoological, geological, and meteorological disharmony to which creation became subject must not be attributed to God. The perfect will of God, as founding King of creation, is not manifest in the presence of death, disease, discord, and disaster any more than it is manifest in human sin. Our present world does not reflect the kingdom order God originally intended for man's enjoyment on earth, nor does it reflect God's kingdom as it shall ultimately be experienced on this planet. Understanding this, we should be cautious not to attribute to "God's will" or to "acts of God" those characteristics of our world that resulted from the ruin of God's original order by reason of man's fall.

Questions:

What Scriptures can you locate that give further insight into the world as God originally intended?

What Scriptures can you locate that describe the "new earth" that will one day be?

✎ _____

_____

Probing the Depths

As God promised, Noah was kept safe throughout all the cataclysmic events of the Flood. But Noah had to experience the unimaginable devastation, the death throes of all people outside the ark, the turbulent chaos of a meteorological and geological maelstrom. He was saved, but he was forced to live through the storm. His life was spared, but the trauma he experienced is unimaginable.

There are those who would have us believe that the righteous do not suffer. The general principle is that those who reverence God will experience well-being, while those who reject God will not prosper; yet observations do not confirm this general principle. Good men have experienced disaster, while the wicked have gone on practicing evil undisturbed. This philosophy of life sometimes is termed the "Deuteronomic formula." (See Deuteronomy 4:40; 5:29, 32–33; 28:1–2.) According to this philosophy, living right and practicing good will result in blessings of prosperity in this life. On the other hand, doing evil will reap only suffering and negative repercussions in this life. (See Deuteronomy 28:15, 58–63.) While the Deuteronomic formula expresses a basic principle of life (we reap what we sow), we know many exceptions exist. Bad things do happen to good people, and the wicked do not always immediately get the punishment they deserve. The book of Job deals with the mystery of the suffering of the righteous. According to Job, this mystery of life's inequities can be surmounted only by faith, not by reason.

Read Matthew 7:24–27.

Questions:

Have you experienced "storms" in your life? What kinds of "storms" were they?

_____

_____

_____

What was your reaction?

_____

_____

_____

How does this story of Noah change your view of the experience?

_____

_____

_____

Deeper Questions:

How have you seen the Lord judge sin in your life or in the life of someone else?

_____

_____

_____

Did He allow sowing and reaping to take its course, or did He intervene directly?

_____

_____

_____

How was the judgment you described above an act of mercy and preservation for the one judged or for others?

_____

_____

_____

A Fresh Start

When the eight members of Noah's family and the army of animals finally stood outside the ark—the only living creatures on the entire planet—it was time for a new beginning. This beginning could not be like the one in Eden because of the presence of sin, so God needed to tell Noah the ground rules for this fresh start and a renewed order is established.

Noah's faith, which occasioned his deliverance, is manifest in an expression of worship to God as he disembarks from the ark. God declares His covenant with Noah after restating His purpose to make man to be fruitful and multiply, as at the beginning.

However, other factors are not as at the beginning, notably the relationship of God with man, as well as of man with creation. The Flood has not reversed the loss of man's original domination. He is still fallen, though thankfully a recipient of God's mercy.

Further, the animals will fear humankind from this time on which was not characteristic of their relationship prior to this. In the ultimate restoration of God's kingdom on Earth, the original fearless order will be regained. (See Isaiah 11:6–9.)

Notwithstanding these deficiencies, a cleansed realm for seeking God's kingdom first is newly available to man, and again God asserts man's responsibility for administering Earth with an accountability to Him. The Flood has not neutralized the influence of the Serpent, nor has it changed humankind's capacity for rebellion against God's rule. Nevertheless, new hope dawns with promise for the eventual recovery of what was lost of his first estate.

Read Genesis 9:1–17.

Questions:

What do you understand to be God's core message here?

✎ _____

_____

_____

_____

_____

As one of Noah's descendants, what does this mean to you?

✎ _____

_____

_____

_____

_____

Behind the Scenes

The descendants of Ham's son Canaan inhabited the land the Lord would promise to Abraham, Isaac, and Jacob. The patriarchs lived in the land of Canaan as strangers and pilgrims, but the Lord assigned the nation Moses led out of Egypt the task of driving the Canaanites out and occupying the land as their own.

Clearly this portion of the Genesis account is intended to show the early beginnings of the spirit of Canaanitish corruption in Canaan, their forefather. The prophetic curse establishes an early point of understanding for the future judgment eventually to be visited in Joshua's time. Of the Canaanites the Lord said, "The land is defiled; therefore I visit the punishment of its iniquity upon it, and the land vomits out its inhabitants" (Leviticus 18:25). Read Leviticus 18, which warns Israel against behaving like the descendants of Canaan. Twenty-four times in that chapter the Lord prohibits various sinful ways of "uncovering nakedness."

Record Your Thoughts

Questions:

What fresh starts has the Lord granted you in your life?

✎ _____

_____

_____

_____

_____

How have you thanked Him?

✎_____

_____

_____

_____

_____

If you were going to plan a special time of thanksgiving to God for all of the fresh starts He has given you for eternity and for this life, what would you do?

✎_____

_____

_____

_____

_____

Why not do it?

✎_____

_____

_____

_____

_____

ADDITIONAL OBSERVATIONS

The Beginning of Nations

Genesis 10:1—11:32

Kingdom Key—*God Loves All*

John 3:16, 19 For God so loved the world . . . the light has come into the world, and men loved darkness rather than light, because their deeds were evil.

The peoples and nations listed in Genesis 10, if traced forward in time and given modern names, might read like a directory of the United Nations today. The listing presents the world as it was in ancient times. But it also reminds us that just as the Flood spread the judgment of God throughout the earth, so the blessings of God on Noah have spread through his descendants, through these nations to the ends of the earth. God made "from one blood every nation" of the world (Acts 17:26), the outcome of His charge to Noah (Genesis 9:1).

The Pledge of Allegiance says the United States is "one nation under God." Given the perspective of Genesis 10, one could almost say that there are "many nations under God." Not that any nation has always served God or brought itself "under" His sovereignty. Far from it. Some have violently opposed God's ways. Nevertheless, this passage implies that God is concerned about the *whole* world; He loves *all* peoples. Likewise, as we survey the many nations of the world today, we need to keep in mind that ultimately we are all part of the same family; we are all descended from the same righteous man, Noah (Genesis 10:32).

Questions:

In what ways does the story of Noah and the ark foreshadow God's redemptive plan for humankind?

_____

_____

What can we learn about how God deals with His people from this story?

_____

_____

_____

How would recognizing that we are all descendants of Noah promote unity in the kingdom of God?

_____

_____

_____

The Descendants of Noah

When Moses wrote the book of Genesis for the Israelites who had just left Egypt to begin life as a nation in the land of Canaan, he wanted them to know the stories that defined them. The story of Noah's family was a crucial one because all nations of the earth descended from his three sons. If Israel was to understand the background of their ancestor Abraham, their Egyptian slave masters, and the wicked Canaanites who awaited them in the promised land, they needed to know about Noah's sons.

Noah's sons are always listed in the same order: Shem, Ham, and Japheth. This repeated order is their order of importance in Old Testament history. Eber, a descendant of Shem, is the person whose name probably is the source of the word _Hebrew,_ a shorthand way of saying "son of Eber." This is why Shem is always listed first among the sons of Noah. Ham (the father of Canaan) is listed next because his descendants would oppose the descendants of Shem. Ham's actions in Genesis 9:22 dishonored his father. This earned him one of the first recorded curses in Scripture. Few of Japheth's descendants figure in the Old Testament, so he is listed last.

The Scattering of the Nations

The genealogies of Genesis 10 do not explain how the descendants of Noah came to scatter. (However, a hint is contained in the name *Peleg* [Genesis 10:25], which literally means "Division.") Regardless of how the dispersal transpired, the nations of Noah's sons covered an immense area ranging from present-day Egypt to Iran and from Saudi Arabia to Turkey, an area of more than one million square miles!

Questions:

Of what personal comfort should it be to you to know that God has kept track of these people in Genesis 10 when secular history easily dismissed them from memory as insignificant?

_____

_____

_____

What importance do these genealogies suggest there is in passing on to the next generation a fear and reverence for the Lord?

_____

_____

_____

Kingdom Life—*He Alone Is God*

In Isaiah 14:12–14 Lucifer (whose name means "Day Star") is credited with making prideful claims which presumed to supplant God's rule with his own and assert his independence from the Most High. Lucifer is a type of Satan; once an angel and now the enemy of all that is of God.

Noah's descendants quickly reverted to pagan ways. Their motivation in attempting to build the tower at Babel sounds much the same as Lucifer's statements in Isaiah 14. They sought to build a tower to the heavens and "make a name for" (Genesis 11:4) themselves. What they intended as a monument to human effort became a symbol of divine judgment on human pride and self-rule.

Read Isaiah 14:12–14; Proverbs 8:13; 11:2; 13:10; 16:18; 29:23; Mark 7:21–23; 1 John 2:15–17.

Questions:

Why is pride so often warned against in Scripture?

_____

_____

_____

In what area of your life do you struggle with pride?

_____

_____

_____

How does pride lead to the assertion of independence from God?

_____

_____

_____

Kingdom Extra

Genesis 11:5 doesn't mean that the Lord was unaware of what the united population of the earth was doing until He happened to make a personal inspection tour. Genesis 11:5 is a turning point in this account like 8:1 is the turning point in the Flood narrative. Genesis 8:1 doesn't imply that the Lord had forgotten Noah's family and the animals. These turning-point verses both mean that when the time was exactly right, the Lord got actively involved in the flow of events.

Behind the Scenes

Babel is a play on the Hebrew verb *balal,* which means "mixed" or "confused." The Babylonians later interpreted *Babel* to mean "the gate of the god." Most scholars link this city with Babylon, which eventually became the fountainhead of all demon worship and finally, in Revelation, becomes synonymous with the final evil city that deifies evil and persecutes God's people (Revelation 18).

Questions:

What are the implications that the events at the Tower of Babel account for the origin of and basis for the sin of racism?

✎ _____

_____

_____

How did the attitude that prompted the building of the tower turn into hatred and suspicion?

✎ _____

_____

_____

How is that attitude manifest in the world today?

✎ _____

_____

_____

Kingdom Extra

To illustrate the division of the nations that occurred during the lifetime of Peleg (Genesis 10:25), Moses repeated the genealogy of Shem in Genesis 11, but he diverged from the one given in chapter 10 after the generation that was at Babel. Fill in the following blanks with the names of successive generations in the family tree of Shem based on the lists in Genesis 10:22–29 and 11:10–26.

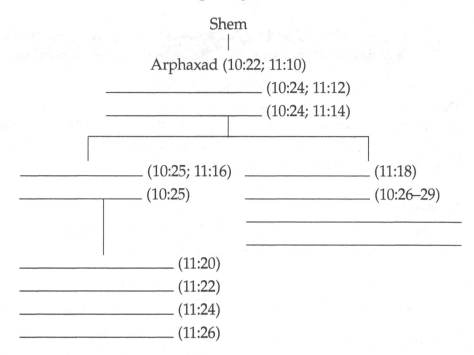

The genealogies of Genesis teach us that lives became shorter and children were born to much younger parents.

A Journey to Destiny

Abram was born in Ur of the Chaldees. It is believed by many that Ur, a pagan nation, was a thriving metropolis boasting a healthy economy and lavish lifestyles. We are not told why Terah, Abram's father, was compelled to set out for the land of Canaan, but he was obviously prompted by a compelling force to set out on such an arduous journey. When Terah settled in Haran, he had traveled more than seven hundred miles. There were still more than eight hundred difficult miles to be traveled before the destination of Canaan would be reached by his son Abram.

Questions:

According to Joshua 24:2, what was the religious orientation of the family of Abram?

When did Abram, the son of a pagan, first hear the call of God (Acts 7:2–4)?

✎ _____

_____

_____

Behind the Scenes

Joshua 24:2 shows that Terah and his forebears "served other gods"; his own name and the names of Laban, Sarah, and Milcah point toward the moon god as perhaps the most prominent of these. Certainly Ur and Haran were centers of moon worship, which may suggest why the migration halted when it did. Terah's motives in leaving Ur may have been no more than prudence (the Elamites destroyed the city circa 1950 B.C.); but Abram had already heard the call of God.

Record Your Thoughts

Life choices can have a profound effect on our tomorrows, but they can also affect the lives of those around us and future generations. Every choice we make involves consequence and repercussion, or benefit and reward, sometimes for generations to come.

From Adam to Noah to Abram, choices have been vehicles of blessing or curse. The same is true in our own lives. We can choose life and blessing and send forth light and life into the lives of our progeny, or we can choose the way of Cain and opt to inflict death and a curse on our descendants for generations to come.

Question:

Reread our KINGDOM KEY for this session. What in these chapters of Genesis brings more power to this powerful truth?

✎ _____

_____

_____

ADDITIONAL OBSERVATIONS

SESSION FIVE

A New Beginning
Genesis 12:1—14:24

Kingdom Key—*Called to Faith*

Matthew 17:20 I say to you, if you have faith as a mustard seed, you will say to this mountain, "Move from here to there," and it will move; and nothing will be impossible for you.

Abraham is designated as the "father" of all who walk his pathway of faith. As such, he is God's revealed example of His plan to eventually reestablish His kingdom's rule in all the earth through people of His covenant. Through Abraham, whom He wills to become "a great nation" (restored rule) and to whom He chooses to give a "great name" (restored authority), God declares His plans to beget innumerable children who will be modeled after this prototypical "father of faith."

Read Genesis 1:26–28; Romans 4:13; 5:17; Revelation 1:4–6.

Questions:

What does it mean to "reign in life" (Romans 5:17)?

✎ _____

_____

_____

Do you experience this in your own life?

✎ _____

_____

_____

Why do you believe this is so?

✎ _____

_____

_____

Word Wealth—*Reign*

Reign: Greek *basileuo* (bas-il-yoo'-o); Strong's #*936*: To reign as a king. This term is used of believers and indicates the activity of life in fellowship with Christ in His sovereign power. Through Jesus' glorious dominion we have been designated "kings and priests" (Revelation 1:6) to God. This is a present calling. These dual offices give perspective on our authority and duty and how we most effectively may advance the kingdom of God.

Kingdom Life—*Follow to Blessing*

It is easy to assume that Abram was raised knowing and serving God. However, we learn from Joshua 24:2 that Terah, Abram's father, not only lived in a pagan Ur, but worshipped false gods. How Abram came to know God is not revealed. But after Terah's death, God spoke directly to Abram.

Genesis 12:1–9 is a pivotal point and marks the beginning of salvation's history. It foreshadows the later patriarchs, the nation of Israel, and the entire Davidic line, including the Messiah. It is also the seedbed for the biblical concept of the blessing—God at work in the lives of His people to counter the effects of the Curse.

Read 2 Corinthians 9:8–14.

Questions:

Is the concept of "blessed to be a blessing" expressed in your life?

✎ _____

_____

_____

What steps can you take to improve the flow of blessing in and through your life?

✎ _____

_____

Sent Forth

The rest of the Bible after Genesis 12 records the spiritual chain reaction set in motion by God when He called Abram to leave Ur of the Chaldeans and by faith enter a covenant relationship with Him. How could such an inauspicious beginning in the household of a pagan named Terah have such far-reaching consequences?

Abram was called by God to give up all that was known and dear to him and journey to a strange land hundreds of miles from all he had ever known, to make a total break with the past and follow Him. This was the first test of Abram's faith.

Question:

What are the implications of Genesis 12:1–3 for you?

✎ _____

_____

Word Wealth—*Abundantly*

Abundantly: Greek *perissos* (per-is-soss'); Strong's *#4053*: Superabundance, excessive, overflowing, surplus, over and above, more than enough, profuse, extraordinary, above the ordinary, more than sufficient. In Genesis we are told that God made everything and declared it to be good. Then He gave this beautiful, plentiful earth to Adam; Adam was given dominion over all of it. God's plan from the beginning was for man to be enriched and to have a prosperous, abundant life.

Kingdom Extra

God is the One who makes all grace abound toward you and provides you sufficiency in all things. All things beneficial for our lives come from God's hands. God provides sufficiency—even "bounty"—so that we might do good works. We are blessed in order to be a blessing to others! (See Genesis 12:2.) The word *sufficiency* means "contentedness" or "competence"—earmarks of the believer whose life is truly blessed by these characteristics as God increases him. And third, the God who gave you seed in the first place is the One who meets your basic needs, multiplies your seeds sown into an abundance you can share with others, and increases you spiritually with love, joy, peace, and all of the other fruits of the Holy Spirit flowing freely in your life—"the fruits of your righteousness" (2 Corinthians 9:10).

How great is our God! We have no lack in Him—only potential! Read Psalms 95; 103:2–5; Romans 12.

Questions:

What bounty do you see in your life that can be shared with others?

✎_____

_____

_____

Do you experience sufficiency in your life?

✎_____

How can this be increased?

✎_____

_____

_____

Kingdom Life—*Faith Pleases God*

Abram's 1,500-mile journey from Ur to Canaan was fueled by faith. Nothing so pleases God as a steadfast faith in all that He is and promises to do. (See Hebrews 11:8–10.)

Read through Genesis 12:4–9 and follow Abram's journey in obedience to the call of the Lord. Note his encounters with the Lord along the way.

Read Hebrews 11:6.

Questions:

Does your degree of faith please God?

✎ _____

How can you increase your faith?

✎ _____

_____

_____

Kingdom Life—*Called to Be Set Apart*

Abram's nephew Lot experienced blessing because of his association with Abram, but Lot did not share Abram's commitment to the call of the Lord. Lot is emphasized in Genesis to help readers understand by contrast what was special about Abram's relationship with God. Genesis 13 illustrates the teaching of Jesus: "Whoever desires to save his life will lose it, but whoever loses his life for My sake will find it" (Matthew 16:25).

Abram's life was set apart for service, worship, and obedience to the Lord. Lot's life continued to be spent in selfish pursuits for personal gain. Blessing followed Abram (Genesis 13:14–17); curse was experienced by Lot. Lot thought he was smart in choosing "all the plain of Jordan" (Genesis 13:11) as his dwelling. He thought he would end up richer and more powerful than Uncle Abram. For the first time (but not the last), Uncle Abram had to rescue Lot. Lot seemed unable to see that Abram's spiritually motivated choices had led to greater power than had his materially motivated ones.

Read Matthew 25:14–29.

Questions:

What do you see as the underlying principle of this parable?

✎ _____

_____

_____

How have you seen this truth illustrated in your experience?

✎ _____

_____

Taken Captive

Love of the world and things of the world can and will bring bonds of captivity. Lot's love of the world had led him to choose to live his life among heathen men—and captivity was the result. He lost all because he guarded his life as his own and refused to turn to the God of Abram. His deliverance was won as a result of Abram's commitment to the Lord. That commitment brought blessing in the form of wealth and might and the ability to aid those in need.

Read Romans 8:7–8; James 4.

Questions:

What things of this world have power to draw you?

✎ _____

_____

In what ways does this interfere with or inhibit your growth in the Lord?

✎ _____

_____

What do you believe Jesus may be telling you about this?

✎ _____

_____

Word Wealth—*Most High*

Most High: Hebrew *'elyon* (el-yohn'); Strong's #5945: Most High, uppermost; pertaining to the heights, in the highest; highness; supreme, lofty, elevated, height in rank, exalted. *'Elyon* is derived from the verb *'alah* meaning "to ascend." It appears as an adjective more than twenty times, describing exalted rulers and even the highest rooms in the wall of the temple (Ezekiel 41:7). It becomes a divine title when paired with one of the names of God, such as *'El 'Elyon* or *'Elohim 'Elyon,* "God Most High." Compare to the angel's declaration at the birth of Jesus: "Glory to God in the highest, and on earth peace, goodwill toward men!" (Luke 2:14).

Melchizedek

We are told that Melchizedek was the king of Salem. (Salem would later bear the expanded name *Jerusalem.*) Abram's seemingly routine encounter with this regional king is revealed centuries later as being an encounter with an antetype of Jesus Christ in His role as priest (Psalm 110:4; Hebrews 7:1–10). *Melchizedek* means "My King Is Righteous or Legitimate," and he greets Abram with a royal banquet of bread and wine. Uniquely occupying the offices of king and priest, he worships God Most High (somewhat of a rarity in the area at that time). Prior to any legal requirement, Abram responds to Melchizedek's office, generosity, and blessing by giving him a tithe of all the spoils gathered in the recent war which freed Lot from heathen kings.

Record Your Thoughts

Questions:

How have you seen faith in the Lord accomplish things that human effort and power could not?

✎ _____

_____

_____

What do you think is the relationship between faith in God and refusal to be allied closely with wicked people?

✎ _____

_____

_____

ADDITIONAL OBSERVATIONS

SESSION SIX

A New Promise
Genesis 15:1—20:18

Kingdom Key—*Believe the Lord*

Mark 9:23 Jesus said to him, "If you can believe, all things are possible to him who believes."

Abram believed in the Lord; he gave full credence to God's Word. This resulted in a legal reckoning. It is the basis for the New Testament teaching that God's way has always been responsive trust in His Word, which then produces right living.

God will respond to our belief in His Word, but that does not grant us the liberty to presume upon God's goodness by irresponsibly asking for selfish things. Our desires must be in accord with God's will. Our hearts must be turned toward God and His plan, as were Abram's.

Read John 1:12; 1 John 5:14–15.

Question:

God spoke and Abram believed. What can we learn from this about receiving in faith?

Kingdom Life—*Protected and Delivered*

God recognized Abram's fear—the fear of leaving no heir. Abram's fear was based on circumstance. Ten years had passed since the Lord brought Abram to

Canaan and promised to give it to him and his numerous descendants. Abram and Sarai began to experience some real doubts about whether God's plan was going to work out. God called Abram to trust based on His promise.

Fear and trust are responses that reflect our heart attitude toward God. Fear grants power to our physical realm; trust acknowledges the power of Almighty God.

Read Luke 12:29–34; Isaiah 41:10.

Questions:

God told Abram, "I am your shield" and "your exceedingly great reward" (Genesis 15:1). What do you understand this to mean?

✎ _____

_____

_____

What does that mean to you in your own life?

✎ _____

_____

How do you live out that truth?

✎ _____

_____

_____

Word Wealth—*Accounted*

Accounted: Hebrew *chashab* (kah-shahv'); Strong's #2803: To think, reckon, put together, calculate, imagine, impute, make account; to lay one's thoughts together, to form a judgment; to devise, to plan to produce something in the mind, to invent. This verb is normally the equivalent of the English "to think," but also contains a strong suggestion of "counting." *Chashab* is the consideration of a number of elements, which results in a conclusion based on a wide overview. In Genesis 15:6, God added up everything that Abram's belief meant to Him and, computing it all together, determined that it was equal to righteousness.

The First Blood Sacrifice Covenant

The direct requirement of a blood sacrifice as the means of establishing a covenant first appears in this episode and God's instruction to Abram. The animals to be offered were selected, cut in halves, and arranged in proper order opposite one another. The covenant parties then passed between the halves, indicating that they were irrevocably bound together in blood. The cutting in halves of the sacrifice spoke of the end of existing lives for the sake of establishing a new bond or covenant. The sacred nature of this bond was attested to by the shedding of life blood. In this instance, only God passed between the pieces, indicating that it was His covenant and He would assume responsibility for its administration. Present in this account of covenant-making are three essential ingredients: (1) a bond that originates from God's initiative, (2) the offering of a blood sacrifice as a requirement of covenant, and (3) God's sovereign administration of the outcome of His oath.

Behind the Scenes

During a most dramatic scene, God humbled Himself to accept the role of the inferior party to this covenant. In the ancient Hittite covenant ceremony, a puppet ruler, the inferior party, would walk between the bleeding pieces of split animals, taking an oath of loyalty to his superior. Here the Lord voluntarily made Himself lower than Abram for the establishment of the covenant. This dramatic act prefigures the precious gift of His own Son, who condescended to die on a degrading cross for all humanity. The Abrahamic covenant is the Old Testament model for the new covenant in Jesus Christ.

In the Abrahamic covenant, the Lord was the promising party. God's oath was unilateral, unconditional, with no requirements demanded of Abram for his part in this mighty covenant. Abram simply believed.

Read John 3:16–17; Luke 22:20; 1 Corinthians 11:25–26.

Questions:

How does this knowledge affect your appreciation of Jesus' sacrifice?

What parallels do you see between this Abrahamic covenant and the new covenant in Christ?

✎_____

_____

Kingdom Life—*Wait upon the Lord*

Sarah was originally called "Sarai," which means "Princess." When God changed Sarai's name to "Sarah," He named her "*The* Princess" or "Queen," linking her in corulership with her husband Abraham (formerly Abram), the "Father of Many Nations," and including her in His covenant promise.

Sarah, the beautiful wife of Abraham, was barren—a condition considered to be a curse in the ancient world. She is a positive lesson in faith that rises above personal limitations. And Sarah's life also reflects the blessing of a submitted spirit that responds biblically to her husband, without losing her own identity or negating her own self-worth.

Sarah is also an illustration of the dangers of taking God's promises into our own hands. Her suggestion that Abraham take her handmaid as wife, in view of Sarah's barrenness, resulted in the birth of Ishmael—a child who occasioned jealousy and conflict between Sarah and Hagar (Ishmael's mother), eventually between their two sons, and to this day, among their offspring.

Read Psalms 27:14; 37:9, 34; Isaiah 40:31.

Questions:

What problem in your life that has seemed to drag on for a long time do you have trouble trusting the Lord to handle according to His Word?

✎_____

_____

What have you done to handle this problem in order to "help the Lord along"?

✎ _____

_____

What is to be gained in your situation by waiting on the Lord and what is to be lost by hurrying Him along?

✎ _____

_____

Kingdom Extra

In Genesis 17:5 God changes Abram's name to Abraham and promises Abraham that he will become the father of many nations. *Abram* means "High Father" or "Patriarch." *Abraham* means "Father of a Multitude." Thus, God was arranging that every time Abraham heard or spoke his own name, he would be reminded of God's promise.

The principle to be learned here is this: let God's words, which designate His will and promise for *your* life, become as fixed in your mind and as governing of your speech as God's changing Abraham's name was in shaping his concept of himself. Do not "name" yourself anything less than God does.

Read Psalm 139:13–18; Matthew 12:34–37; Romans 9:20.

Questions:

What are some typical comments you make about yourself?

✎ _____

_____

How does this limit you in living out God's best in your life?

✎ _____

_____

In what way might this self-deprecation be sinful?

✎ _____

_____

Behind the Scenes

The act of circumcision was required as a sign of the covenant previously established with Abraham. This was not a new covenant but an external sign that Abraham and his descendants were to execute to show that they were God's covenant people. The fact that this was performed upon the male reproductive organ had at least a twofold significance: (1) the cutting away of the foreskin spoke of the cutting away of the fleshly dependence, and (2) their hope for the future posterity and prosperity was not to rest upon their own ability. Circumcision was a statement that confidence was being placed in the promise of God and His faithfulness rather than in their own flesh.

Circumcision was not uncommon in the ancient Near East, but God chose it as a sign to identify the people of the Abrahamic covenant for it literally touches the male at his point of propagating life. Later, pride made circumcision into an idolatrous symbol, which the Hebrews assumed would demand God's continued favor. Just as Christian baptism without faith is meaningless for justification, so it is with mere physical circumcision.

Kingdom Life—*Do Not Doubt*

Both Sarah and Abraham reacted with questioning when God told them that they would bear a child in their old age. Yet there was a distinct difference. Abraham "fell on his face and laughed" (Genesis 17:17) when God told him of Isaac's future birth. Sarah laughed to herself when she overheard the Lord's messengers speak to Abraham of the impending birth of their son. Abraham raised the question in his heart as he spoke to God. Sarah expressed disbelief that such a thing would or could happen. The difference may seem slight, but the effect is in total contrast. Abraham spoke in his heart to God in total transparency. Sarah reacted with total disregard for the message of the Lord. Both laughed; one turned to the Lord for clarification, and the other turned inward with disbelief.

Questions:

What makes the difference between a doubt like Abraham's (Genesis 17:17) that drives a person to the Lord and a doubt like Sarah's (18:12, 15) that pulls a person away from Him?

✎ _____

_____

_____

What things in your life have confirmed that nothing is "too hard for the LORD" (Genesis 18:14)?

✎ _____

_____

Partnership with God

While God was confirming to Abraham and Sarah that the time was ripe for the next generation of the people of promise to be born, the time was also ripe for the birth of the last generation of people of perversion in Sodom and Gomorrah. Ironically, Lot, who had come to Canaan in association with the people of promise, now was identified with the people of perversion.

The Lord honored Abraham by telling of His plan to destroy the evil cities of Sodom and Gomorrah. Urged on by his compassion, his sense of justice, and his faith, Abraham tenaciously questioned God. In the end, his concern for his nephew led him to boldly suggest that God not destroy the cities if ten righteous people could be found. Abraham demonstrated the principle of partnership with God as he felt his way forward in faith.

Read Hebrews 4:16; 11:6.

Questions:

What principle is demonstrated in Abraham's conversation with God?

✎ _____

_____

_____

What heart attitude is at the root of this principle?

✎ _____

_____

How can you employ this same principle in your own life?

✎ _____

_____

Kingdom Extra

At least three important principles emerge in chapter 18 from God's conversation with Abraham. (1) We learn that wicked Sodom could have been spared for the sake of only ten righteous people. From this we learn that it is not the presence of evil that brings God's mercy and long-suffering to an end; rather it is the absence of good! (2) Although God sometimes inspires us to pray by showing us things to come (v. 17), our intercession must be in line with God's character and covenant with men. Like Abraham, we may appeal to God (v. 25) to preserve His name, honor, and perfect justice before the world. (3) Although we often measure influence by numbers, man's arithmetic cannot be used to estimate the impact of the righteous. God saves by many or by few.

The Seduction of the World

Lot had chosen to live amid wicked and sinful people as a result of his desire for and attraction to the things of the world. Although he had begun his journey in the presence of Abraham's great faith and doubtless knew much about God and His plan for His people, Lot allowed love of the world to draw him into an unhealthy alliance with sin.

The results were devastating. The virtue of hospitality flared into a vice of incredible behavior when Lot offered his daughters as a means of protecting his guests. The love of possessions caused him to choose to linger when destruction was imminent. In choosing to escape into a nearby city rather than into the mountains as the angels instructed, Lot exhibited his dependence on and attachment to worldly things. And Lot's daughters, operating out of fear and godlessness, chose sin rather than prayer or investigation of their perceived isolation.

Read Proverbs 22:8; Matthew 6:24; Galatians 6:7–8; James 1:12–15.

Questions:

How does the pull of the world affect your life today?

✎ _____

How does this affect your walk with the Lord?

✎ _____

_____

_____

What steps can you take to lessen the effects of worldly desires?

✎ _____

_____

_____

God Is Faithful to His Promise

On the very night "the son of promise" was to be conceived, the Lord had to preserve Sarah, "the mother of promise." Man of faith that Abraham was, he still had some bad habits—customs picked up, perhaps, from his pagan father—that got him into trouble. But God acted immediately to preserve Sarah in spite of Abraham's deceptive actions in attempting to hide his true relationship with her (Genesis 20:1–17).

It is important to note, however, that Sarah was, indeed, Abraham's half sister. But she was his "sister" in another manner also. While in Haran, it is entirely possible that Abraham had availed himself and Sarah of the local custom of "adopting" one's wife as sister in order to confer special privileges, including inheritance, upon her.

Nonetheless, Abraham's deception of Abimelech stands in stark contrast to God's sovereignty.

Read Psalm 32:7–10; Isaiah 52:12; 2 Thessalonians 3:3.

Questions:

Have you ever experienced God's deliverance from a situation you caused?

✎ _____

_____

_____

What does this tell you about God's character?

✎_____

_____

_____

What can you learn from this story about the promises of God?

✎_____

_____

_____

Behind the Scenes

Abimelech is a title rather than a proper name, just as *Pharaoh* is a title rather than a name. All the kings of the Philistine city Gerar apparently used *Abimelech* as a public title. *Abimelech* meant "My Father, the King," and its use showed respect and reverence on the part of his subjects. In Genesis 26 Isaac and Rebekah will use the same ploy about their identities with King Abimelech of Gerar. But readers cannot tell whether Isaac dealt with the same Abimelech as Abraham or another king of Gerar with the same title. If they are different kings, they are both presented as upright rulers.

Record Your Thoughts

Questions:

Relate an incident in which the Lord protected you from your own folly so that you could carry out His plans for your life.

✎_____

_____

Abraham had to learn over and over that the Lord did not want him to use deception as a means of self-protection. What is a spiritual or moral lesson that you have found hard to get into your behavior pattern even though the Lord has taught it to you over and over?

✎_____

_____

SESSION SEVEN

The Son of Promise

Genesis 21:1—24:67

Kingdom Key—*God's Promises Are Sure*

2 Corinthians 1:20 For all the promises of God in Him are Yes, and in Him Amen, to the glory of God through us.

We live in a dysfunctional world. Words are separated from context, making it possible to create new meanings for almost any word ever spoken. Words change in their meanings, sometimes drastically so. It is vitally important to put your faith in the Promiser—the Lord Himself—as opposed to putting your faith only in the promises. Being a part of this dysfunctional world, we are prone to take precious promises meant for kingdom purposes to further our own agendas.

It is important that we fully understand why Abraham's experience in faith is so important. He *heard* a *promise*—and he believed *in the Lord.* Never allow the *promise* to be separated from the *One who has made the promise!*

Read Hebrews 10:23 and 2 Peter 1:2–4; locate other Scripture passages that assure you God will perform His promises.

Questions:

How can you guard against placing more importance on the promise than the Promiser?

How can recognition of God's faithfulness help in this regard?

✎ _____

_____

_____

When have you experienced God's faithfulness in providing what He has promised?

✎ _____

_____

What effect has this had on your own faithfulness?

✎ _____

_____

_____

A Son Is Born

God's promise to Abraham and Sarah that they would bear a son was fulfilled in Isaac. In actuality, Isaac was the assurance that all the promises God had made to Abraham would be fulfilled. Imagine the joy they experienced in this incredible event. Imagine also how such a miracle would strengthen your faith.

The name *Isaac* means "Laughter." Sarah named Isaac in the midst of her joy-filled laughter at his birth. She seemingly forgot laughter when the angels predicted that she would bear a son in her old age.

Isaac was born into a family surrounded by the spiritually hostile culture of the Canaanites. The Canaanites were a godless society filled with idolatry and immorality. Yet Abraham remained faithful to God and raised Isaac to serve the Lord.

Kingdom Life—*Trust in the Lord*

As a result of Sarah's impatience and disbelief, she convinced Abraham to father a child through her maid Hagar. Untold trouble began with her attempt to take matters into her own hands.

Ishmael seemingly disliked Isaac and scoffed at him (Genesis 21:9). The Hebrew word translated as "scoffing" can mean "playing," "laughing," or "reproaching." In Galatians 4:29, Paul used the word *"persecuted"* in describing Ishmael's treatment of Isaac. Whatever the treatment, Sarah was highly offended on her son's behalf and convinced Abraham to send Hagar and Ishmael away.

The consequence of Sarah's lack of trust in the Lord is paid yet today with the continual conflict between the descendants of Isaac and Ishmael.

Read Psalms 37:3–5; 118:8; Proverbs 3:5–6; Isaiah 46:9–11.

Questions:

Is there a promise from the Lord for which you are still waiting?

In what way have you attempted to help God bring a promise to fruition?

What was the result?

Probing the Depths

Examples of single parents throughout Scripture offer encouragement and hope to those facing similar situations. Hagar stands as a key example of someone who has been unfairly treated, deserted, and cut off with little provision. Yet, in Hagar's life, we see the Lord intervening with spiritual and physical provision. Other examples throughout Scripture show the Lord supporting single-parent situations with provision, deliverance, restoration, and instruction. God also promises to take the place of the spouse/parent who is absent (Isaiah 54:4; Hosea 2:19–20; Psalms 10:14; 68:5; 146:9) and to be available to help parents who find themselves alone (Exodus 22:23; Hebrews 13:5b).

Probing the Depths

Listening to Sarah's voice had originally been folly for Abraham, just as it had been for Adam when he listened to Eve. But in the case of Hagar and Ishmael, God says in effect to Abraham, "Listen to her. She is speaking My truth." (See Genesis 21:12.)

Sarah had grown and matured since that earlier fateful day when she suggested that Abraham take the fulfillment of God's promise into his own hands. Her name (nature) had been changed, a symbolic foreshadowing of the new birth in Christ. God had clarified that His original plan was still in place—His covenant promise would be fulfilled through Abraham and Sarah together.

God has never veered from His original design—man and woman working together to increase His kingdom on the earth. A woman's effectiveness multiplies when she is confident that she has a powerful place in the ongoing purposes of God and as her husband affirms this.

Kingdom Life—*Hold to the Promises of God*

A vision from God must often first die, and then the Lord resurrects the vision from its ashes. Such was the case with the vision God had given in regard to Isaac's and Abraham's innumerable progeny.

God called Abraham to take Isaac to "the land of Moriah" (Genesis 22:2). It is believed this is the same place that would come to be called Mount Zion, the location of the temple in Jerusalem. There he was to offer Isaac as a burnt offering to God. A burnt offering belonged entirely to God and no share was allowed to any man.

While it is not clear exactly why God chose to ask for a human sacrifice (a practice He clearly forbids in Deuteronomy 18:10), the main point is obviously the test of Abraham's faith.

We are told in Hebrews that Abraham "received him [Isaac] in a figurative sense" (11:19) as raised from death. Abraham so believed God that he trusted that, even if Isaac died that day on the altar, God would not negate His promise. He knew in his heart that God would fulfill His promise even if it meant Isaac must be resurrected.

Read Hebrews 11:1.

Questions:

With the story of Abraham and Isaac in mind, how do you now understand this verse?

✎ _____

_____

How does your faith measure up in view of Abraham's unswerving belief?

✎ _____

_____

What steps can you take to arrive at a greater level of faith?

✎ _____

_____

What has the Lord ever asked you to give up for His sake to reveal your character?

✎ _____

_____

From your experience, give an example of surrendering something to God only to receive it back better than ever.

✎ _____

_____

_____

Word Wealth—*Only Son*

Only son: Hebrew *yachid* (yah-cheed'); Strong's #3173: An only one, an only child, a precious life. *Yachid* comes from the verb *yachad,* "to be one." *Yachid* describes Abraham's unique miracle child, Isaac. Zechariah describes what the Messiah will one day become to Israel's repentant, weeping citizens: a precious only son (Zechariah 12:10). Here the place where God told Abraham to sacrifice his son Isaac is the same place where God sacrificed His own Son many years later: the hills of Moriah in Jerusalem. Equally noteworthy is that the phrase "His only begotten Son" in John 3:16 in the Hebrew language is "His Son, His *Yachid.*"

The Image of Faith

Abraham's ability to lead was tested in three areas of faith: (1) *Faith to risk* (Genesis 12:1–5): a wealthy man, Abraham risked all to follow God. The godly leader is willing to risk everything on God's faithfulness and venture into the unknown. (2) *Faith to trust* (17:1–27): Abraham and Sarah were long past the age of childbearing. The godly leader does not rely on facts alone but goes beyond facts to faith. (3) *Faith to surrender* (22:1–19): Abraham knew the sacrifice of his son would destroy any hope of fulfilling God's promise that he would father many nations. The godly leader is willing to sacrifice all things precious in order to please God.

Questions:

The apostle Paul was one of the greatest leaders the church has ever known. In what ways were these qualities apparent in his life?

_____

_____

_____

How are these qualities lived out in your own life?

_____

_____

_____

The Next Generation

A great tragedy in the family of Abraham was the death of Sarah. In spite of Abraham's great wealth, the field and cave at Hebron where Sarah was buried were all the land he ever owned in Canaan. Yet this purchase proved Abraham's confidence in God's promise for Isaac and future generations. Up until this point Abraham described himself as "a foreigner and a visitor" (Genesis 23:4) in Canaan. After this purchase, Abraham gained for himself and his descendants a permanent holding in Canaan.

After Sarah's death, Abraham turned his attention to locating a wife for Isaac. It was time for Isaac to start his family to further the growth of the people of promise. Abraham was ready to relinquish front stage in the drama of redemption to Isaac and his descendants.

Kingdom Life—*The Rewards of a Servant's Heart*

In obedience to his master's wishes, Eliezer followed the directions he was given to the letter. His reward was locating Rebekah.

Rebekah was a Syrian, the granddaughter of Nahor, Abraham's brother. Her name refers to "tying or binding up," implying that her beauty was so great it could literally "captivate" or "fascinate" men. She is introduced as a diligently industrious and beautifully sensitive girl with a servant's heart. Her willingness to serve Eliezer and her readiness to draw water for all ten of the thirsty camels dramatize this.

A lesson in the way God provides surprising rewards for servant-spirited souls is seen in what happened to Rebekah. Little did she know the camels she willingly watered were carrying untold gifts for her and her family.

Read Matthew 20:27–28; Mark 9:35; 10:43–44.

Questions:

Have you experienced the rewards awaiting a servant spirit in your own life? Explain how.

✎ _____

_____

What other Scripture portions can you find that instruct you to be servant-minded?

✎_____

_____

_____

_____

Record Your Thoughts

Questions:

What promises has the Lord spoken to your heart that remain to be fulfilled?

✎_____

_____

_____

What about this story of Abraham increases your ability to wait on the Lord for a promise's fulfillment?

✎_____

_____

_____

Who has the Lord prepared to be a special blessing in your life as surely as He prepared Rebekah for Isaac, and how has that person blessed your life?

✎_____

_____

_____

What can you learn from the habit of grateful worship by Abraham's servant that could help your spiritual life?

✎_____

_____

_____

Selfishness in the People of Promise

Genesis 25:1—31:55

Kingdom Key—*Humility Is Key*

Philippians 2:3 Let nothing be done through selfish ambition or conceit, but in lowliness of mind let each esteem others better than himself.

Those who observe a godly life see what God is like. This is one of the church's primary functions. Godliness avoids anything that brings disunity or division in the church. It lives unselfishly, making others the primary focus of its concerns.

Read Romans 12:10; Galatians 5:26.

Questions:

When do you find it difficult to "esteem others better than" (Philippians 2:3) yourself?

_____

_____

_____

What effect does envy, jealousy, emotional pain, or personal trial have on your ability to consider others first?

_____

_____

_____

How can you overcome these self-centered tendencies?

✎ _____

_____

_____

Faith vs. Selfishness

Whether we like to admit it or not, the experiences of Abraham's family closely parallel our own human experience. As we follow the story of this all-too-human family, look closely at the contrasts of faith with selfishness. Against the shining backdrop of the faith of Abraham, Isaac, and Jacob, though called to the covenant of the Lord, plays out a sometimes distressingly selfish drama of family intrigue.

Self-protection can be the prudent action of a wise man or it can be the scheming wile of a fox. Note all the variations between the two extremes of self-protection in Genesis 25 and 26.

Probing the Depths

It is often observed how certain tendencies appear in families generation after generation. It is striking to note how frequently behaviors and circumstances are repeated within a family tree. In reading through these chapters of Genesis, note the similarity of Rebekah's experience to Sarah's; the relationship of Esau to Jacob as compared to the relationship between Ishmael and Isaac. Consider what attitudes and actions were results of learned behavior.

Behind the Scenes

The names of Isaac and Rebekah's twin boys had meaning, as did most Hebrew names. The name *Esau* was suggested by the baby's hairy appearance. While the name *Esau* does not mean "Hairy," it sounds like the word that does and so suggests that meaning.

Jacob, an existing name found elsewhere, means "May He Be at the Heels" or "May God Be Your Rear Guard." But it also lends itself to a hostile sense of dogging another's steps, or overreaching (literally,

"Supplanter" or "Deceitful"), as Esau bitterly observed in Genesis 27:36. Through his own actions Jacob devalued the name into a synonym for treachery.

Kingdom Life—*God Has a Plan for Your Life*

The saga of intrigue between Jacob and Esau came as no surprise to God. In Romans 9:10–13 we are given insight into God's plan which began before these twins were ever born: "When Rebecca also had conceived by one man, even by our father Isaac (for the children not yet being born, nor having done any good or evil, that the purpose of God according to election might stand, not of works but of Him who calls), it was said to her, 'The older shall serve the younger.' As it is written, 'Jacob I have loved, but Esau I have hated.'"

God's choice of Jacob instead of Esau was not based on anything either had done or would do in the future. It was solely based on God's election, His purpose and plan. God is never unjust in dealing with people. As sovereign Creator, He has the right to deal with people according to His will, whether it is in the exercise of His compassion or His wrath.

It is important here to realize that "loved" and "hated" are not to be understood in their normal sense. They are best understood as "chose" and "rejected," based on the fact that God knew Jacob would better further His will for His people.

Read Jeremiah 1:5; Psalm 139:13–17; John 6:44.

Questions:

How do you know that you have been "chosen" by God?

✎ _____

_____

Since God chose you, what does this say about His opinion of you?

✎ _____

_____

In what ways can you further God's plan for His people?

_____

_____

_____

Word Wealth—*Birthright*

Birthright: Greek *prototokia* (pro-tot-ok'-ee-ah); Strong's #4415: *Prototokia* is the right or advantages of the firstborn son. The single occurrence of this word is found in Hebrews 12:16 in reference to Esau. The firstborn son received a double portion of the inheritance along with preeminence and authority as the father's heir. Connected to the birthright of the line of Abraham was the honor of being in the lineage of the Messiah. Esau transferred his birthright to Jacob for a paltry bowl of stew, profanely despising his spiritual privilege. In the history of the nation, God occasionally set aside the birthright to show that the objects of His choice depended not on the will of the flesh, but on His own authority. Thus Isaac was preferred to Ishmael and Jacob to Esau.

Jacob's Ladder

It is interesting to note the dream that brought Jacob to knowledge of God involved a ladder. Ladders are used to reach elevated destinations, to arrive at points that are beyond our grasp. And so it was with this dream. This encounter marks the beginning of Jacob's personal relationship with the Lord.

Jacob's dream emphasizes God's initiating grace as He assures Jacob He is the Lord of the past and future. Jacob was the third generation to receive the promises of the Abrahamic covenant, not because he was righteous, but because of God's call and faithfulness to Abraham. Since Jacob had probably never heard God's voice before, the Lord identified Himself by His prior relationship with Abraham and Isaac.

Although Jacob's response in Genesis 28:20–22 may sound cynical or even as if he is attempting to bribe the Lord, such is not the case. Jacob was endeavoring to grasp the promise and to adopt the Lord as his God by formalizing a relationship such as his father had enjoyed.

This was a pivotal point in Jacob's life as he began a personal relationship with the Lord.

Read Matthew 5:13–15.

Questions:

What circumstances marked the beginning of your relationship with the Lord?

✎ _____

_____

_____

What people in your life have been instrumental in your understanding of the things of the kingdom? In what specific ways?

✎ _____

_____

_____

How might you be used to increase the kingdom awareness of others?

✎ _____

_____

_____

Kingdom Life—*The Lord Disciplines His Own*

Although Jacob was God's choice to be heir and patriarch, Jacob's actions in dealing with his family reveal a heart filled with envy, pride, and deceit. But God had a plan to purify Jacob's heart.

Laban was Rebekah's brother, Jacob's uncle. Jacob had every reason to trust that Laban would have only his best interests at heart. But Jacob found his match in Laban and, through him, tasted the effects of a cunning and deceitful heart. Jacob was tricked by his uncle into marrying two of his cousins when he loved only one of them. Jacob then experienced the consequences of being on the receiving end of deception in the form of strained relations between his wives.

Jacob also learned that our sins have a way of catching up to us. Jacob had pretended to be Esau in order to deceive his father. He found himself deceived in much the same way when Leah was encouraged to pretend to be Jacob's true love, Rachel. Jacob's deceit of Isaac had been his mother's idea, and Jacob discovered to his grief that Laban was just as scheming and dishonest as his sister Rebekah.

Laban was obviously God's means of discipline in Jacob's life, and Jacob spent twenty years learning humility and grace. In the end, Jacob's tenacity won his heart's desire—God's reward for a lesson well learned.

Read Hebrews 12:5–11.

Questions:

In what ways have you experienced God's "chastening" (Hebrews 12:7) or discipline in your life?

✎ _____

_____

What was the outcome?

✎ _____

_____

Leah

Jacob never loved Leah. But God saw her pain and responded by blessing her with children while Rachel remained barren. Even in her emotional distress, Leah praised God. God's love for Leah was made evident as each son was born to her. She became the mother of the priestly and kingly tribes of Levi and Judah.

The Levites would one day be given the honor of serving as priests in the house of God. Their important tasks would give the world a picture of the redeeming work of the coming Messiah.

The name *Judah* means "Praise," and from this child a great tribe of Israel would be born. He would one day receive the highest blessing from his father in which he would be told that royal authority, legal authority, and honor of being in the lineage of the Messiah would be his.

List all the sons of Leah and of her maid Zilpah. Next to each, list the meaning of the name.

✎ _____

_____

_____

_____

_____

Rachel

Although Rachel was dearly loved by Jacob, she remained childless for many years. She looked on as Leah presented four sons to Jacob and praised God with the birth of each. It is not made clear in Scripture why God chose to keep Rachel barren, but one wonders if her attitude might have been a major contributing factor.

Barrenness was cause for great shame in biblical culture. It was a sign of God's displeasure. In desperation to end her shame, Rachel attempted to take matters into her own hands and offered Jacob to Leah for the night in exchange for mandrakes collected by Leah's son Reuben (Genesis 30:14–16). (Mandrakes are a fragrant plant with small yellowish fruit. They were considered to be an aphrodisiac and were reputed to induce fertility.) Rachel's scheming was obviously faithless and resulted in further shame and disappointment when Leah was the one who conceived following this ill-fated plan. Only God could help Rachel.

Finally God allowed Rachel to conceive and bear a son to Jacob. She would later bear Jacob's youngest son and die in childbirth. (See Genesis 35:16–18.)

List the sons born to Rachel and to her maid Bilhah. Next to each, list the meaning of the name.

✎ _____

_____

_____

_____

_____

Behind the Scenes

Laban continued to cheat Jacob, but God's blessings are always able to exceed man's evil ways. Jacob was blessed exceedingly by God and left the house of Laban with his family and great possessions. But it would have been better had Jacob trusted God to provide a way of escape rather than attempt to flee in fear from Laban.

As Jacob prepared to leave Laban's home, Rachel stole Laban's household gods. These gods (called *teraphim*) were small figurines and held great meaning to the heir of the household. According to the ancient law around Haran (where Laban lived), the sons, particularly the eldest, had the privilege of inheriting the family gods, as well as all the property that went with them. Rachel stole the figurines from Laban either to ridicule his religion, to lay claim to the inheritance, or to remain attached to her native religion.

Considering the childless state with which she suffered for years, one wonders if Rachel's heart attitude is displayed in this act of theft.

Record Your Thoughts

Questions:

Why is it hard for scheming people to have friends?

_____

_____

_____

_____

Why do people close to schemers tend to become schemers themselves (as did Rachel)?

_____

_____

_____

_____

Like everyone else, schemers reap what they sow. What built-in judgments do you think scheming people face?

In their families:

In their friendships:

In their working relationships:

ADDITIONAL OBSERVATIONS

Hatred in the People of Promise

Genesis 32:1—36:43

Kingdom Key—*Love Is Essential*

1 John 3:14 We know that we have passed from death to life, because we love the brethren. He who does not love his brother abides in death.

God is love. Love is the central, quintessential description of the nature of God. God's love for man seeks to awaken a responsive love of man for God. Divine love runs like a golden thread through the entire Bible. There we discover God giving Himself and all He possesses to His creatures in order to win their response and to possess them and share Himself with them.

Love is the high esteem God has for His human children and the high regard they, in turn, should have for Him and other people. Love is not only one of God's attributes; it is also an essential part of His nature. God is the personification of perfect love. Such love surpasses our powers of understanding. Love like this is everlasting, free, sacrificial, and enduring.

Love can only be known from the actions it prompts. It is like oil to the wheels of obedience. When God imbues us with His love, we are enabled to run toward Him and to desire to follow His commands and to live out His will in our lives.

Love expresses the essential nature of God and found its perfect expression in the Lord Jesus.

Read 1 Corinthians 13; 1 John 4:7–19.

Questions:

In whom have you seen God's love made manifest to the world? How was God's love made evident?

✎ _____

_____

_____

What difference have these lives made in the world?

✎ _____

_____

_____

Is love an attribute that others recognize in you?

✎ _____

_____

_____

What difference might you make in your world if you love others as God loves you?

✎ _____

_____

_____

Kingdom Life—*Peace Is God's Will*

Jacob was terrified at the prospect of facing Esau again. He had plotted and schemed to acquire the birthright and as he faced the prospect of seeing Esau, he devised schemes to appease his brother's wrath. Fortunately, the Lord intervened to draw Jacob's attention to His presence and protection.

God desired that Jacob not only find peace with his brother, but that peace would flood his heart as he entered into a trusting relationship with his Lord.

Read Isaiah 26:3; Philippians 4:6–7; Colossians 3:14–15.

Questions:

What is the peace of God?

_____

_____

_____

What are the blessings that attend a peaceful heart?

_____

_____

_____

Do you experience God's peace in your own life?

_____

_____

_____

Word Wealth—*Peace*

Peace: Greek *eirene* (eye-ray'-nay); Strong's #*1515*: A state of rest, quietness, and calmness; an absence of strife; tranquility. It generally denotes a perfect state of well-being. *Eirene* includes harmonious relationships between God and men, men and men, nations, and families.

Peace: Hebrew *shalom* (shah-loam'); Strongs #7965: Completeness, wholeness, peace, health, welfare, safety, soundness, tranquility, prosperity, perfectness, fullness, rest, harmony; the absence of agitation or discord. *Shalom* comes from the root verb *shalam*, meaning "to be complete, perfect, and full." Thus *shalom* is much more than the absence of war and conflict; it is the wholeness that the entire human race seeks.

Wrestling with God

"Then Jacob was left alone; and a Man wrestled with him until the breaking of day" (Genesis 32:24). This is one of the Bible's most mysterious narratives. The Man is identified in Hosea 12:4 as an angel. The importance of the narrative is Jacob's willingness to contend with God at his time of desperate need. He knows God has willed to bless him, and he will settle for nothing less than his full inheritance. His contending tenacity causes him to prevail.

The angel required that Jacob state his name. Obviously, the angel knew his name, but Jacob was made to say it because of its meaning— "Supplanter" or "Deceiver." Jacob had to acknowledge his weakness before he could later be transformed from Jacob to Israel.

The name *Israel* can mean "Prince with God," "He Strives with God," or "May God Persevere." In spite of Jacob's character weaknesses, God commends him for his prevailing attitude. Jacob is a fighter. As such, he is a model to be emulated whenever we face difficulty or a need for character transformation.

Kingdom Life—*To See God's Face*

In boldness of faith, Jacob engaged God fully (wrestled with Him) that God would fulfill His promise to bless him and cause him to be a blessing to the families of the earth.

The idea of wrestling with God in prayer does not mean man twists God's arm to get Him to act, but rather that human passion evidences the desire for what He has promised. God gave Jacob the ultimate answer to his prayer: He showed Jacob His face. This encounter so changed Jacob's life and perspective, he could now see the face of God! To see God's face in a life-transforming encounter is the goal of every prayer. God wants to reveal the knowledge of His glory by the power of His Spirit in the face of Jesus Christ. It is worthy to ask, seek, and knock as we persistently pursue the Father for deeper works of the Holy Spirit.

Read Deuteronomy 4:29; Luke 11:9–10; 2 Corinthians 4:6.

Questions:

How have you experienced persevering prayer?

What has been the outcome?

_____

_____

How did this experience transform your life?

_____

_____

_____

A Harvest of Hatred

It must have seemed wonderful to Jacob when he had survived the hurdle of encountering Esau and was settled in the land promised to him by the God of his fathers, Abraham and Isaac (Genesis 28:13–14). Soon he found that his greatest danger was not from external enemies but from the harvest of hatred springing up in his family from the seeds of selfishness.

In dealing deceitfully with those who had raped their sister Dinah and scheming to exact retribution, Jacob's sons endangered the entire family. Jacob's family was forced to flee from the danger and establish a new home. Only the "terror of God" (Genesis 35:5) protected them as they ran from the men of Shechem to Bethel. This may have been a natural disaster, a plague, or simply a great fear of the sons of Jacob. The expression "terror of God" normally indicated some kind of catastrophe attributed to the Lord. Even in the midst of hatred and vengeful anger, the Lord continued to protect His chosen ones.

However, hatred and disregard for one another continued to plague the family of Jacob. Jacob's eldest son, Reuben, showed total contempt for his father when he took Jacob's concubine as a lover. Although the repercussion was slow in coming, this indiscretion later cost him his birthright.

Behind the Scenes

Jacob seemed often to follow the course of least resistance and failed to confront people and situations that were sinful and harmful. Whether he acted from a feeling of unworthiness to speak truth or an unwillingness to stand strong for right, his failure often compounded bad situations.

This behavior is common today. Whether in the name of tolerance, to avoid seeming petty or judgmental, or out of some personal fear, we choose to walk in a deceptive peace.

If we are to be lights to the world, we must speak truth. If we are to be salt, we must bring to bear God's truth into sinful and harmful situations. We cannot hide from confrontation if we truly desire to live out the life of God's kingdom.

Read Colossians 3:16–17; 2 Timothy 3:16–17.

Questions:

What are the spiritual and personal dangers posed when you avoid dealing with major conflicts with other people?

✎ _____

_____

_____

How can this be harmful to those around you?

✎ _____

_____

_____

In your own life, when has confrontation resulted in a more godly relationship?

✎ _____

_____

_____

Kingdom Extra

Complete the following chart to get an overview of the altar-building that the patriarchs engaged in as they wandered as pilgrims in the promised land.

GENESIS	PATRIARCH	PLACE	NAME OF GOD
12:6–7			
12:8			
13:18			
22:2, 9			
26:23–25			
33:18–20			
35:1, 7			

The God whom the patriarchs worshipped by means of these altars in the book of Genesis wants to be known. God is not a distant, uninterested deity, but a loving Father who wishes to be known by the children of His heart.

Look up the following passages and note other names by which the Lord revealed Himself in Genesis.

14:18–22	
16:13	
17:1	
21:33	
31:42, 53	
49:24	

Kingdom Life—*You Will Have Trials*

Kingdom people experience trials, suffering, and not always instant victory. Triumph and victory may characterize the attitude of each citizen of the kingdom of God, and Holy Spirit–empowered authority is given to be applied to realize results. Yet God did not promise life without struggle. The dominion being recovered through the presence of the King within us and ministered by the Holy Spirit's power through us is never taught by the apostles as preempting all suffering.

Victory comes only through battle, and triumph follows only trial. To be an overcomer, one must face an obstacle. Only a weak view of the truth of the kingdom of God pretends otherwise. Another weak view surrenders to negative circumstances on the proposition that we are predestined to problems and therefore should merely tolerate them. The Bible teaches that although suffering, trials, and all other sorts of human difficulty may be unavoidable, all may be overcome. The presence of the King and the power of His kingdom in our lives make us neither invulnerable nor immune to life's struggles. But they do bring the promise of victory: provision in need, strength for the day, and healing, comfort, and saving help.

Read Romans 8:37–39; Acts 14:22; 2 Thessalonians 1:3–5; James 1:2–4.

Questions:

What do you understand to be the purpose of the trials in our lives?

_____

_____

_____

_____

What have been some points of victory in your own walk with the Lord?

_____

_____

_____

_____

What benefits have you experienced?

_____

_____

_____

_____

Record Your Thoughts

Questions:

How has the Lord made His sustaining presence known to you during times of distress?

✎ _____

_____

_____

_____

_____

What places, times, or events in your life function as Bethel did for Jacob—things to go back to physically or spiritually for renewal and strengthening?

✎ _____

_____

_____

_____

_____

ADDITIONAL OBSERVATIONS

A Savior for the People of Promise

Genesis 37:1—41:57

Kingdom Key—*Pride Is Destructive*

Proverbs 16:18 Pride *goes* before destruction, and a haughty spirit before a fall.

If pride is the greatest sin—and it is—then humility must be the greatest virtue. It is humility that allows us to acknowledge that God has a claim on our lives, that we are fallible, mortal creatures, and that God is the Master of the universe. It is humility that says, "I am a sinner, and I need to be saved." Humility is the beginning of honor (Proverbs 22:4). The truths of the kingdom are perceived only by those who are humble. No one who is proud will ever gain anything from God. Those who are humble receive the grace of God and are given the secrets of the kingdom, because they come as beggars.

Read Matthew 5:3; James 4:6; Proverbs 22:4.

Questions:

In what areas of your life do you struggle with pride?

_____

_____

What has resulted from these areas of sin?

_____

_____

What does true humility look like?

✎ _____

_____

_____

How can you appropriate these traits in your own life?

✎ _____

_____

_____

Kingdom Life—We Are Shaped by God

We know that Jacob loved Joseph more than his other sons, even favoring him to the point of bestowing upon him a robe that may well have been the type worn by royalty. Joseph may well have been a spoiled child with a feeling of entitlement. It is obvious his brothers hated him.

As a teenager, Joseph wasn't ready to be a family savior. Then as now, it took suffering to produce a saint who could have dramatic impact on other people.

Read Romans 5:3–5.

Questions:

In what ways has the suffering of the past changed you?

✎ _____

_____

_____

How are you now more prepared for ministry and life in the kingdom?

✎ _____

_____

_____

A Life Call

The Hebrew word for "had a dream" (Genesis 37:5) means "to bind firmly" (Strong's #2492). Joseph became firmly bound up in the dream that God had given him. Dreams that are from God are spiritual experiences that take root deep in your hearts, never to be forgotten. Joseph had a dream, but perhaps we could more accurately say that the dream had Joseph! The dream would sustain him through all that would happen to him over the years. Like Moses, he "endured as seeing Him who is invisible" (Hebrews 11:27).

Questions:

What do we learn about young Joseph as he shares his dreams with his family?

✎ _____

_____

How do these same traits appear in your own life?

✎ _____

_____

Behind the Scenes

The merchants who purchased Joseph as a slave are called both Midianites and Ishmaelites (Genesis 37:28). Technically Midianites were descendants of Abraham's son by his second wife, Keturah (25:1), and Ishmaelites were descendants of Abraham's son by Hagar, Sarah's Egyptian maid (25:12–18).

Ishmaelite seems to have been an all-inclusive term for Israel's nomadic cousins. It is used much as the word *Arab* is used today in speaking of any of numerous tribes of people.

Judah: Portrait of a Traitor

Judah occupies an important role in Hebrew history. We learned earlier that *Judah* means "Praise," but there was little praise due him as he sold his young brother into slavery, an act that was a type of kidnapping and punishable by death. (See Exodus 21:16 and Deuteronomy 24:7.)

His actions later in life remained callous, deceitful, and merciless. Although he had promised his sons' widow, Tamar, that he would give her to his youngest son, Shelah, he reneged on his word. This would have condemned Tamar to life as a childless woman, a state that was considered a curse by ancient peoples.

There seemed to be no hint in Judah's character that he might be open to the action of God's Spirit to use him as an instrument of blessing. Yet God had already set in motion a plan whereby Judah's heart would be softened and his life transformed. No one is beyond the saving grace of God.

Read Psalm 53:1–3; Romans 3:10–18, 23.

Questions:

What differences do you see in your character before and after you received God's saving grace?

_____

_____

_____

What then should be your response to those who live godless lives?

_____

_____

_____

Word Wealth—*Signet*

Signet: Hebrew *chothemeth* (kho-the-meth); Strong's #2858: A signature seal, used to ascertain the source of a document or proclamation. A *chothemeth* was a personal identification seal hanging from a cord about its owner's neck.

Tamar had a sense for the dramatic. She obviously planned her clandestine manipulation of Judah in advance. When she asked for his signet as his pledge of payment, she knew his identity could not be hidden. Anyone in Judah's household would quickly identify Judah's seal.

Kingdom Life—*Purified by Suffering*

Joseph went through a series of difficulties that would have broken a person who had no faith in God. These experiences purged away the youthful boasting of a father's favorite son. But through these experiences, God's protective hand remained on Joseph's life.

Having been beaten and reviled and ultimately sold into slavery by his brothers, Joseph found himself in an alien culture at the mercy of Potiphar, a wealthy man who had purchased him as a slave. When wrongly accused of attacking Potiphar's wife, Joseph suffered imprisonment in irons and chains. (See Psalm 105:18.) He should have been executed since the penalty for such a crime would have been death. His imprisonment shows God's providence and hints that Potiphar may not have fully believed his wife.

God had a massive task ahead for Joseph and used the circumstances of his life to discipline him and prepare him.

Read Proverbs 13:24 and Hebrews 12:5–6, 11.

Questions:

When have you experienced the Lord's loving discipline in your life?

_____

_____

_____

In looking back, for what situation was He preparing you?

_____

_____

_____

How should we perceive the Lord's chastening or discipline?

_____

_____

_____

The Reward of Integrity

No matter the trial he faced, Joseph remained faithful to God. His heart remained unstained by anger or bitterness. His view of being sold into the slavery that resulted in his imprisonment was that he had been unjustly "stolen away" (Genesis 40:15). This took all the blame off his brothers.

Throughout Joseph's imprisonment, he operated with compassion, integrity, and wisdom. His sensitivity to others led to his interpretation of two dreams and paved the way to his release from prison and rise to power in the very kingdom in which he was enslaved.

Read Psalms 7:8–9; 26:1–3; 41:9–12; Proverbs 10:9; 11:2–3.

Questions:

What does it mean to walk in integrity?

_____

_____

_____

_____

Is this something others would recognize in you?

_____

_____

_____

If not, how might this be remedied?

_____

_____

_____

Kingdom Life—*Enabled to Serve*

When the Lord knew that Joseph was spiritually ready to handle the task He had for him without pride, the Lord brought Joseph to a position of power. From that position Joseph would humbly save multitudes of starving people from many nations.

It is in just such a way that God prepares each of us to minister in the kingdom. Just as Joseph recognized his ability to interpret dreams came from God, we can only minister effectively as we recognize our ability to do so comes strictly through His enabling. It is only by the power of the Spirit of God working in and through our lives that God's power is made manifest through His people—the gold of His life in vessels of clay.

When we recognize our inability and embrace God's preeminence, we can walk in His power. Then and only then can we experience the impact of Philippians 4:13: "I can do all things through Christ who strengthens me." It was true for Joseph and remains true today—when God calls, He enables.

Questions:

How has God supernaturally enabled you to go beyond your own limitations?

✎ _____

_____

What effect has this had on your faith? On the faith of others?

✎ _____

_____

Behind the Scenes

Dreams were assumed to be messages from God. (See Job 7:14.) The ancient Egyptians left many hieroglyphic writings with detailed instructions on how to interpret dreams; thus the magicians and wise men were experienced in understanding what God was telling Pharaoh. The magicians were expected to be experts in handling the ritual books of magic.

Record Your Thoughts

The outline of God's restoration work stands out vividly in the life of Joseph. Joseph was *forsaken, falsely accused,* and *forgotten.* But finally he was *favored* by God and restored to the rule God had ordained for him.

Questions:

From your observation, how does God generally prepare His children for major responsibilities in the church or other Christian organizations?

_____

_____

Why is pride such a difficult spiritual enemy for leaders, especially young ones like Joseph?

_____

_____

If the Lord doesn't take a believer through suffering, how else might He teach that believer to be humble?

_____

_____

In what areas of your life do you continue to struggle with pride?

_____

_____

How does this affect your ability to serve effectively?

_____

_____

Rescue for the People of Promise

Genesis 42:1—45:28

✝ Kingdom Key—*God Is Redeemer*

Isaiah 48:17 Thus says the LORD, your Redeemer, the Holy One of Israel: "I am the LORD your God, who teaches you to profit, who leads you by the way you should go."

Redemption is God's providential care of His people. To be redeemed is to be ransomed, repurchased, and set free. It is the process of exchange through which that which is lost through helplessness, poverty, or violence is restored.

The biblical view of redemption is extremely wide, for God has pledged to redeem the whole of creation, to end the bondage and set all captives free.

Read Psalm 107:1–7; Isaiah 43:1; John 8:34–36; Galatians 5:1.

Questions:

In what ways have you experienced God's redemptive plan in your life?

✎ _____

_____

How may God redeem time? Relationships? Opportunities?

✎ _____

_____

Put in your own words what it means to be redeemed.

✎ _____

_____

_____

Restoration

The family of Israel had been torn asunder by pride, envy, and malice. Joseph's brothers were held captive by past sin and guilt, and they had no way of seeking forgiveness or reconciliation. But God had set in motion a plan whereby relationships could be restored and all that was lost could be reinstated.

What Joseph's brothers had meant for evil, God used for good. When the seven-year famine struck, God had placed Joseph in a position of power. His godly wisdom and obedience to God saved untold numbers of people. Joseph's brothers were forced to come to him as the controller of the only adequate food supply in the region.

Thus God set in motion events that would lead to healing and restoration for the family of Israel. When God operates in the lives of men, His purposes are multilayered and multidimensional. Even the sinful actions of men can be used by God to bring about His perfect plan.

Read Joel 2:25–27.

Questions:

What does it mean that God will restore the years the locust has eaten?

✎ _____

_____

_____

How have you experienced this in your own life?

✎ _____

_____

_____

Kingdom Life—*Confront Your Sin*

The ordeal brought to bear by Joseph against his brothers was not vindictive. It was God's means of awakening their consciences so that they would acknowledge their guilt and repent.

On their first trip to Egypt, Joseph's brothers were faced with the anguish they had put Joseph through. On the second trip, they had to confront the decades of grief they had caused their father, Jacob, by letting him think that Joseph had been killed by wild animals.

Read Matthew 5:23–24; James 5:19–20.

Questions:

When has the Spirit of God brought back to your memory a sin hidden in your past that He wanted you to deal with?

_____

_____

_____

How did the Lord bring your forgotten guilt to your attention?

_____

_____

_____

What did He want you to do to deal with that guilt?

_____

_____

_____

Word Wealth—*Reconciled*

Reconciled: Greek *katallasso* (kat-al-las'-so); Strong's #*2644*: To change, exchange, reestablish, restore relationships, make things right, remove an enmity. Five times in the New Testament the word refers to God's reconciling us to Himself through the life, death, and resurrection of His Son, Jesus (Romans 5:10; 2 Corinthians 5:18). Whether speaking of God and man, husband and wife, or the healing between brothers, *katallasso* describes the reestablishing of a proper, loving, interpersonal relationship that has been broken or disrupted.

Judah's Sacrificial Offering

As the last of Joseph's arranged trials is uncovered, Judah stands in humble representation of his brothers. From this moment there can be no doubt that Judah is the leader of the sons of Israel.

Although Joseph desired the welfare of his family, he did not trust his brothers. He was still working through his hurt and his role as God's agent of healing and restoration. Nevertheless, he wished to bring his family to Egypt where they would be safe and cared for.

Judah's impassioned plea for Benjamin's release broke Joseph's heart. At this point, forgiveness flowed freely and reconciliation began. Judah's love for his father and brother and his willingness to sacrifice his own life were instruments of healing for the entire family of Israel, a graphic foreshadowing of the love of the coming Messiah.

Questions:

What other events in the life of Joseph give us insight into God's plan of redemption for humankind?

_____

_____

_____

Why do you think substitutionary love is so spiritually powerful in helping people respond to God?

_____

_____

_____

Tell of an instance in which you have seen Christian love motivate someone to take on himself or herself the burdens, misfortunes, or punishment of someone else in order to help that person.

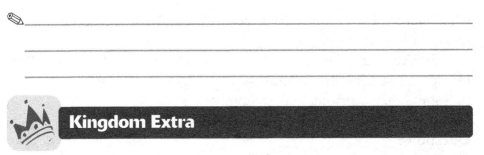

Kingdom Extra

The story of Joseph is an early account of the forgiving nature God expects us to display in our treatment of those who have wronged us. It is a founding example of Christlike love.

Joseph's forgiveness of his brothers' sin is so complete that he kisses all of them and weeps with joy at being united with them once again. Brotherly love is expressive, self-giving, and offered in a way that assists its being received.

Love embraces those who have wronged us and will "cover a multitude of sins" (1 Peter 4:8).

Read 1 Peter 4:8.

Questions:

How can love cover sin?

When have you experienced this in your own walk with the Lord?

Record Your Thoughts

Forgiveness is not the spiritual grace you exercise toward people who annoy you or who accidentally offend you. Forbearance is the old-fashioned term for the grace that you need to direct at them

(Colossians 3:13). Forgiveness is bestowed on people who betray you and are disloyal to you.

Frankly, there are many Christians who refuse to forgive. They take perverse pleasure in nurturing grudges, unaware that they are poisoning their spiritual lives (Hebrews 11:15).

Questions:

What sorts of offenses do you find it hard to forgive the offender?

_____

_____

_____

What sorts of offenders do you find hard to forgive?

_____

_____

_____

What did you learn about forgiveness from Joseph's treatment of his brothers that can help you be more forgiving?

_____

_____

_____

SESSION TWELVE

A Promise of Peace

Genesis 46:1—50:26

Kingdom Key—*God's Peace Is Sure*

John 14:27 Peace I leave with you, My peace I give to you; not as the world gives do I give to you. Let not your heart be troubled, neither let it be afraid.

We learned earlier that peace is much more than lack of conflict. It is an inner tranquility that recognizes God's love and His power. Peace is God's will for all creation. It is to be in total harmony: complete, perfect, and full. Peace is the wholeness that the entire human race seeks.

Read Psalms 4:8; 29:11; 34:14; 119:165; Proverbs 12:20.

Questions:

How does one pursue peace?

✎ _____

_____

_____

What is a "counselor of peace" (Proverbs 12:20)?

✎ _____

_____

_____

Do you experience true peace in your own life?

✎ _____

_____

_____

Why do you believe this is so?

✎ _____

_____

_____

Kingdom Life—*Wisdom Comes from God*

Through suffering the Lord had made Joseph wise, and Pharaoh had recognized this wisdom when he made Joseph administrator of the food collection and distribution system in response to the divinely forecast famine. The Spirit of God had energized Joseph's wisdom in his sanctifying encounters with his brothers when they came to Egypt with the mundane goal of buying food. Finally, Joseph directed his wisdom toward advancing the welfare of his family and the reign of Pharaoh.

Read Psalms 51:6; 111:10; Proverbs 2:1–10; 1 Corinthians 1:24–25.

Questions:

What is your definition of wisdom?

✎ _____

_____

How can wisdom be gained?

✎ _____

_____

What are the benefits of wisdom?

✎ _____

_____

_____

Kingdom Extra

Jacob never ceased worshipping and serving God, even through heartbreak and loss. Such was his security in the Lord that he stood before Pharaoh, whose power was unlimited, and spoke a blessing as he would over a son.

God's blessing was on Jacob's life, even when events seemed otherwise. Pharaoh conferred upon Jacob and his clan the "best of the land" of Egypt (Genesis 45:18).

Questions:

How can wise adherence to the ways of God as revealed by His Word and Spirit lead to prosperity for a child of God, even when the times are difficult?

How can a long and intimate walk with the Lord give you confidence to face the powerful people of the world with the ease and authority that Jacob displayed in the presence of Pharaoh?

Jacob's Final Blessing

The Lord allowed Jacob several years in which to enjoy the flourishing of his family in Egypt. When his time to die came, Jacob blessed his descendants out of a heart at peace with God and his children. The Lord had prepared Jacob through a great deal of heartache to see into the future of his offspring by means of the Holy Spirit.

Genesis 49:1–28 records Jacob's final words to his sons in which he distills all that he has learned about them through the years and all that the Lord has revealed to him about their future. Summarize the meaning of Jacob's poetic predictions about each of his sons.

Reuben

Simeon and Levi (See Genesis 34:25–31.)

_____

_____

_____

_____

Judah

_____

_____

_____

_____

Zebulun

_____

_____

_____

Issachar

_____

_____

_____

Dan

_____

_____

_____

Gad

_____

_____

_____

Asher

✐ _____

_____

_____

Naphtali

✐ _____

_____

_____

Joseph

✐ _____

_____

_____

Benjamin

✐ _____

_____

_____

Kingdom Life—*Trust in God*

The final paragraphs of the book of Genesis portray an intimate level of fellowship and communication among the members of Jacob's family. Where there had once been suspicion and jockeying for advantage, there was now openness and companionship.

The life of Joseph powerfully displays God's sovereign ability to bring to pass His destiny for an obedient individual. Through Joseph we learn these important truths:

- *Ponder God's vision.* Do not share it prematurely, but ask God for His timing.
- *Expect God's favor in the sight of others.* God is able to make a way even when it seems impossible.

- *Remain faithful to God in all you do.* Do not compromise, especially when the vision is slow in coming.
- *Believe that God is sufficient.* He has given you the gifts you need to realize His purpose through you.
- *Trust in God's sovereign providence.* He causes all things to work for your good as you remain faithful to His calling and purpose for you.

Read Proverbs 3:5–6.

Questions:

What vision has God given you that has not yet come to pass?

✐_____

_____

_____

How does the story of Joseph speak to that situation?

✐_____

_____

Record Your Thoughts

Questions:

Why were Jacob and his sons able to trust one another after years of suspicion and dishonesty?

✐_____

_____

_____

What truths from the example of Jacob and his sons can you apply to your life with your family and your church to make those relationships closer?

✐_____

_____

_____

As you look back over your study of the book of Genesis, what spiritual lesson stands out to you as the main truth the Lord wants you to remember and how should you apply it to your life?

_____

_____

_____

Conclusion

We can understand Genesis only if we grasp the truth of original sin and its consequences in our lives and in our relationship with our Creator. Only a Savior can deal effectively with this inherited natural corruption.

God's promises hold true yesterday, today, and forever. He has made a way for us to know the relationship He created us to have with Him. From Genesis to Revelation, His love is made known and His plan made clear.

Probing the Depths—*Review*

Review the KINGDOM KEYS we have studied throughout this study of the book of promises and beginnings: Genesis. Write in your own words what each aspect means to you in your walk with the Lord.

1. God Created All Things

_____

_____

_____

2. All Have Sinned

_____

_____

_____

3. God Is Just

_____

_____

_____

4. God Loves All

_____

_____

_____

5. Called to Faith

_____

_____

_____

6. Believe the Lord

_____

_____

_____

7. God's Promises Are Sure

_____

_____

_____

8. Humility Is Key

_____

_____

_____

9. Love Is Essential

_____

_____

_____

10. Pride Is Destructive

✎ _____

_____

_____

11. God Is Redeemer

✎ _____

_____

_____

12. God's Peace Is Sure

✎ _____

_____

_____

Consider how each of these points is lived out in your life. Do your actions and attitudes convey to the world that you believe your God *is* God?

"You send forth Your Spirit, they are created; and You renew the face of the earth" (Psalm 104:30).

ADDITIONAL OBSERVATIONS